ALL AROUND LAMBEG

Historical Walks

Exploring

LAMBEG

BALLYSKEAGH

TULLYNACROSS

SEYMOUR HILL

CONWAY

HARMONY HILL

BELSIZE

BELFAST ROAD

HILDEN

QUEENSWAY

Fredrick Gilbert Watson

FREDRICK GILBERT WATSON

for Cara, Katie, Emily and Sophie

"Out of monuments, names, words, proverbs, traditions, private records and evidences, fragments of stories, passages of books that concern not story, and the like, do save and recover somewhat from the deluge of time."

The Advancement of Learning   FRANCIS BACON 1605.

First Edition
First Impression

© Fredrick Gilbert Watson and Colourpoint Books 2008

Designed by April Sky Design, Newtownards
Printed by: GPS Colour Graphics Ltd, Belfast

ISBN 978 1 906578 15 2

Colourpoint Books
Colourpoint House
Jubilee Business Park
21 Jubilee Road
Newtownards
County Down
Northern Ireland
BT23 4YH
Tel: 028 9182 6339
Fax: 028 9182 1900
E-mail: info@colourpoint.co.uk
Web-site: www.colourpoint.co.uk

Contents

THE NEIGHBOURHOOD OF LAMBEG – circa 1935

With the walks described indicated in red.

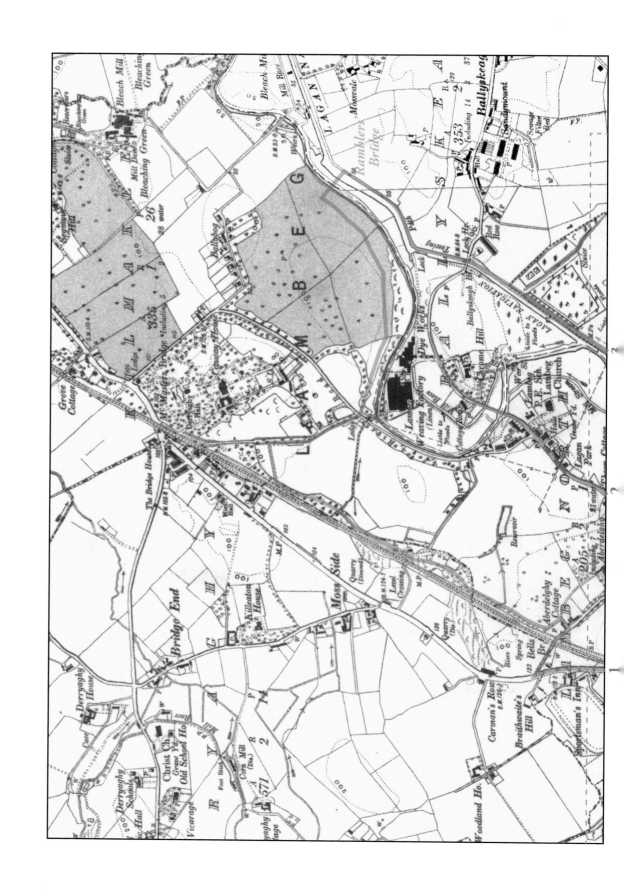

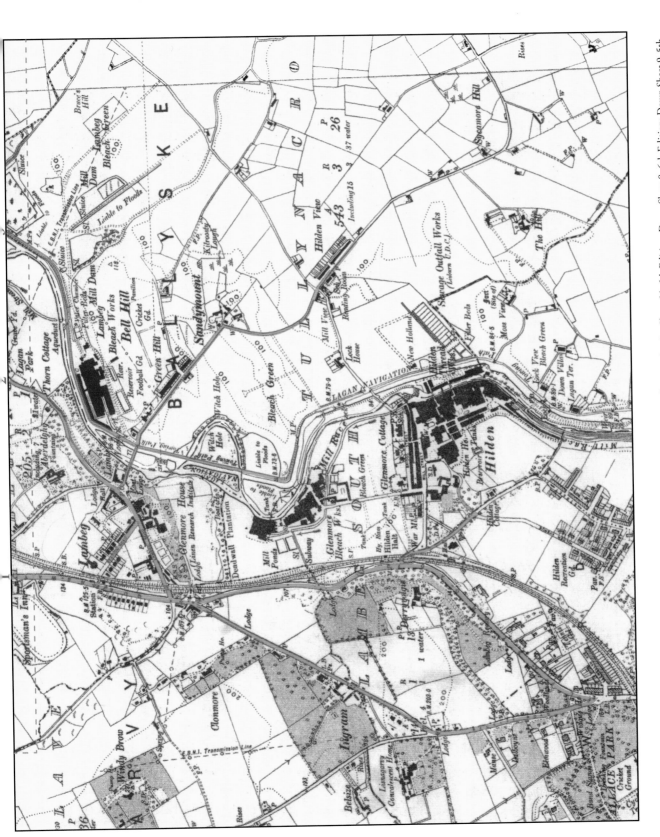

This map was created by combining parts of the following Ordnance Survey of Northern Ireland Six Inch maps: Antrim Sheet 64, 6th Edition; Down Sheet 8, 6th Edition; Down Sheet 9, 5th Edition. Reproduced from the 5th and 6th Editions of the Six Inch Land and Property Services/Ordnance Survey of Northern Ireland map. Map shown here slightly reduced from the scale originally published. Approximate scale of this map 1:11,060.

0   1 kilometre

1 mile

ACKNOWLEDGEMENTS

I would like to acknowledge the many people whose co-operation and assistance contributed greatly to the compilation of this book. In particular I would like to thank Trevor Parkhill of the Ulster Museum and Anne Robinson of the North of Ireland Family History Society who not only read the script and offered advice, but gave words of encouragement at the outset, and John Parkinson who helped at a later stage.

I would also like to thank those who so generously shared with me the results of their own research: Alison Muir, Robert Heslip, Linde Lunney, Winifred Glover, Victor Hamilton, Brian Curry, Alister McReynolds and Brenda Collins. I am appreciative of the help given by the staff of the Linen Hall Library; Lisburn Library; Belfast Central Library; the Public Record Office of Northern Ireland, the Environment and Heritage Service: Built Heritage, the Plunkett Foundation, English Heritage, the Ulster Medical Society and the Rolls-Royce Foundation.

I am grateful to the following for providing much useful information and giving permission to use photographs; Edna Mulligan, Elise Coburn, Dame Mary Peters, Robin Charley, Helen Spence, Samuel Cullen, Patrick Corkey, David Fletcher, Debbie Ormerod, Rankin Armstrong, William Parker, Simon Clay, Karam Ram, Bob Price, John Kelly, William Chittick, Terence Robinson, Richard Bryson, Heather Kenny, Derek Johnston, May Blair, Thomas Muir, Charles Rosenfield, Mrs H. McCabe, the McConnell family and Rev. Kenneth McReynolds. Many others provided me with additional information or snippets of information that proved useful leads to other areas of research. Among them were John McCabe, Raymond Cullen, Ed McClarnon, John Herron, Joe Fitzgerald, Norah Boyle, Rev Hugh P Kennedy, Very Rev. Canon George O'Hanlon, Dawson Stelfox, Eric Irwin, Nelson Bell, Dr Ben Simon, Jack Larkin, Linsay Hunter, Herbert Meeke, David Anderson, Sean Adair, Jim Connaghan, Paul Parkes, Tom Turkington, Jack McKinstry, Pat McCorry, William Waring, Margaret Rossbottom, Harry Wright, James McFarland, Jim Mc Farland, John de Campi, Sheila Duckworth, Mervyn Ferguson, Mark Hagan, Ronnie Campbell, Phil Brooks, Anthea Mc Williams, Nancy Irwin, Mat and Jean Crothers, Douglas and Myrtle Savage, Jim and Roberta Pithie, Gerard Murphy, Mrs Kirkwood, Mr Veale, Tom Kerr, William Orr and members of Lisburn District Orange Order.

My especial thanks are due to the Irish Linen Centre and Lisburn Museum Curator, Brian Mackey and his staff for their assistance and support, in particular Trevor Hall and James McAlister. The help and advice of Norman and Wesley Johnston of Colourpoint Books was much appreciated. On a sad note, I recall a pleasant and informative day spent at Lambeg and Hilden in the company of the late Jim Moloney and I record my appreciation of his interest in my work and the support that his memory generated.

I wish to record my thanks and appreciation to those listed below who provided generous financial support towards the costs of this publication:

Irish Agricultural Wholesale Society Ltd
Lisburn City Council
Lisburn Arts Advisory Committee

Eleanor Wolfenden-Orr
Coca-Cola Bottlers (Ulster) Ltd
Zirkus Creative

FG Watson   March 2008

FOREWORD

In comparison with many of the civil parishes in the Lagan Valley, or further afield, Lambeg is a relatively small parochial unit of only five townlands, yet it has through its industries 'a big history' of remarkable interest. The townlands of Lambeg North and South indeed contained one of the greatest concentrations of the industrialised linen industry to be found in Ulster. William Barbour's mills at Hilden and the neighbouring Richardson, Sons and Owden bleach works at Glenmore were respectively claimed by their owners at the end of the nineteenth century to be "the biggest linen-thread mill in the world" and "the largest bleaching establishment in Ireland".

In the mid 1960s, when a young boy, I bicycled from south Belfast along the Lagan canal towpath to visit a relation who lived in one of the then new houses at Harmony Hill. On the way, I can still recall my wonder at seeing for the first time the red sandstone high bridge at Ballyskeagh, and the enormous scale of the red brick mass that is Hilden Mill. Some years later, when I began my curatorial career in Lisburn, I was drawn again to the roads and narrow laneways around Lambeg and, by car or on foot, visited and explored the places I was learning about through historical research. If only then I had possessed a guide such as *All Around Lambeg* to accompany me, my discovery and understanding of this area's past would have been much more complete.

Much has changed in the Lambeg area in recent decades, with the demise of the linen industry and the building of new housing. Linen is no longer to be seen spread on the greens at Glenmore or Seymour Hill, nor the mill horn to be heard at Hilden but fortunately much of the great mill complex has survived and may now find new uses to preserve its landmark status.

With such a fascinating area, it is especially important to understand and appreciate what has made it what it is, not least so we can respect and conserve what we can of its immense character. Gilbert Watson is to be commended for this study of the Lambeg area and for sharing his knowledge with us in such a friendly way. For anyone living or working in the greater Lisburn area, interested in how the past has shaped our surroundings, this is a book to read and enjoy.

Brian Mackey
Irish Linen Centre & Lisburn Museum

KEY TO PHOTO CREDITS

BNL   Belfast Newsletter

ECA   Emily Charley Album

EHS   Environment & Heritage Service

ILC & LM   Irish Linen Centre & Lisburn Museum

JAK   JA Kelly, Esq

JDHT   Jaguar Daimler Heritage Trust

PRONI   Public Record Office of Northern Ireland

SCC   Samuel Cullen Collection

Zirkus   Zirkus Creative

Colour photographs are by the author unless otherwise stated.

Thanks and acknowledgements are due to the Controller of Her Majesty's Stationery
Office and the Deputy Keeper of the Records, Public Record Office of Northern
Ireland for permission to reproduce photographs.

CHAPTER 1

Lambeg Village

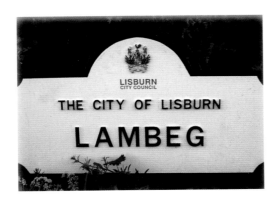

Welcome to Lambeg and environs. Without wishing to beat the drum, I would suggest that the word Lambeg is familiar to most people in Northern Ireland. However, having said that, detailed information on the location, character, residents, industry and history of the village of that name and the immediate neighbourhood may not instantly spring to everyone's mind. It is hoped that this presentation of short historical walks may serve as a guide to those residents and visitors who are interested in, or curious as to, what has gone before, and an *aide memoire* to those who already have an awareness of the rich and varied history of this area.

We will begin by exploring the Lambeg village area and our starting point at Harmony Hill Presbyterian Church is chosen for convenience. The old part of the village is located on the opposite side of the main road behind the railway embankment carrying the Belfast to Dublin railway line. Before we proceed, we first pause at the junction of the Moss Road with the Belfast to Lisburn road, and to the right of the railway bridge, through which the road runs to Lambeg, you will see another arch, which is boarded up. This was the west entrance to Glenmore House and, round about 1840, the owner, James Nicholson Richardson, engaged the architect Thomas Jackson, to replace the gate lodge at this entrance and another at the east entrance.[1] Both gate lodges have been demolished and on this occasion, and on future occasions, we must rely on a photograph to convey a sense of the past. Cross the road and enter the village by passing under the bridge.

Others have passed this way and recorded their observations on Lambeg and in an age of enlightenment. Two Friends who shared this modern view were John Rogers and Elizabeth Doyle, a teacher at Friends' School, whose marriage became a test case supported by the reformers. Neville Newhouse in *A History of Friends' School Lisburn* describes the events leading up to the marriage, which took place in a room in the school in March 1801.

> They were quite willing, perhaps eager, to allow themselves to be the test case which John Hancock's party were seeking. So they sent a letter to Lurgan Monthly Meeting, stating that they wished to marry without "going through a round of formal ceremonies." It was, they boldly claimed, in the interests of simplicity and truth that they made their suggestion. The Meeting however refused their request and sent two of their members to visit the couple and discuss matters with them. Neither side being willing to give way, the visit achieved nothing. Lurgan Meeting insisted that there must be the formal appearance, while the parties concerned refused to make them. Neither would they marry in a church with a priest, even though, as religiously inclined people, they wanted some kind of simple service. They solved their dilemma by marrying in a room in the school on Prospect Hill.
>
> From a Quaker point of view this is the most dramatic single happening in the school's long history.[33]

Local Friends, including John Hancock and some of the school's senior pupils, witnessed the marriage. The adults were disowned by the Society, and George Thompson, the schoolmaster, although he did not attend the ceremony, was dismissed from his post for allowing the use of a schoolroom. These controversies led to a schism within the Society referred to as the Quaker Separation, although no new separate grouping was formed. John Hancock wrote pamphlets stating his reasons for withdrawing from the Society, which were published in Ireland, England and America. He retained his reforming zeal and his life style continued to be modelled on Quaker principles.

Belfast Monthly Magazine

John Hancock, together with William Drennan and John Templeton, were the proprietors of the *Belfast Monthly Magazine*, a journal that ran from 1808 to 1814, and served as the mouthpiece of liberal opinion in the Belfast area. We are mainly concerned with Mr Hancock but some brief comment on his fellow correspondents is appropriate. Dr William Drennan, (1754–1820), was the son of a Presbyterian Minister, physician, poet, educationalist, co-founder of the United Irishmen, and political radical; he is credited with the first reference, in print, to Ireland as the 'Emerald Isle'. John Templeton (1766–1825), from a prosperous Belfast merchant family, married Katherine Johnson of Seymour Hill, sister to Margaret, the wife of the Lisburn-born leader of the United Irishmen, Henry Munro. A United Irishman, the friend of Thomas Russell, a naturalist and botanist with a considerable reputation, he discovered the first specimen of red broomrape (*Orobanche alba*) in the British Isles, on Cave Hill in 1793.[34] He suggested the establishment of a botanical garden in Belfast as early as 1807. Templeton was born at Orange Grove, so named because William III was entertained there on his way from Carrickfergus to the Boyne. He changed the name of the family home to Cranmore and the ruins of the house, and part of a plantation of exotic trees created by him, are located in school sports grounds beside the Malone Road, Belfast.

The three proprietors, comprising a Presbyterian, an Anglican and a Quaker, collectively promoted and championed liberal principles and causes in the *Belfast Monthly Magazine,* which required courage and commitment in the period following the '98 Rebellion, the Act of Union, Robert Emmet's failed insurrection in 1803 and, in the same year, Thomas Russell's trial and execution at Downpatrick. It has been suggested that John Hancock was for a while the editor of the *Magazine.* He is named on its pages, and he was the author of many articles under the pseudonym 'K'. The contributors appealed for civil and religious liberty, advocated better conditions for Roman Catholics and supported Catholic emancipation. The Orange Societies were perceived as an organisation that tended to separate Ireland from England and Catholic from Protestant.[35] Hancock was the Secretary of a society called The Friends of Civil and Religious Liberty, which took a decision to present an anti-orange petition before both Houses of Parliament.[36] This led to some strong protests against the *Belfast Magazine* in the correspondence columns of the *Belfast News Letter.* The final letter in the series claimed victory: "the *Belfast Magazine* is no more … the good sense of the country could no longer tolerate that pestilent publication." [37]

We must not regard John Hancock as an Irish Nationalist; on the contrary, he regarded national prejudices as folly and maintained the English policy in Ireland was desirable to ensure commercial progress.[38] Less controversial, but influential, were the anti-war articles, those on behalf of ex-prisoners, the spread of paper currency, criticism of parental slackness, the abolition of slavery and the reduction of capital punishment offences. Education was a focal topic throughout the life of the publication and Hancock expressed his views clearly: "parents make an erroneous calculation, who in the allotment of their time and attention, prefer to give the bent of their minds to make their children rich, or adorned only with superficial accomplishments, while the more valuable acquisitions of a liberal and guarded education are neglected." [39] The proprietors were to the forefront in lay support for the Belfast Academical Institution. When the Institution was opened on 1 February 1814, William Drennan echoed their thoughts in his address by stating that its primary purpose was "to diffuse useful knowledge, particularly among the middling orders of society, as one of the necessaries rather than of the luxuries of life." [40]

The Camp on Vinegar Hill,
by George Cruikshank.

Rebellion

During the 1798 rebellion, John Hancock, Jacob Martin and Samuel Woodcock, all members of the Society of Friends from Ulster Province, were taken prisoner by the rebels while on a visit in the region of Enniscorthy, Co Wexford. They were taken to the insurgent camp on Vinegar Hill where they were questioned and most were set at liberty. Hancock, however, was held at the camp for two days and made to attend mass, but he was permitted to remain standing with his hat on, according to orthodox Quaker practice.[41] John Hancock later described the proceedings as "an awful spectacle, to see so vast a multitude, many in a state of brutal intoxication, and their arms yet reeking of the blood of their fellow-creatures, presuming to invoke the God of Peace to pour a blessing on their recent acts, and to prosper the ferocious designs they were still harbouring against their unoffending countrymen."[42] In the *Belfast Monthly Magazine*, John Hancock, in referring to the state of Wexford in 1798, saw "important lessons of instruction both to the people and to the rulers", he continued …

the former may see danger of resisting established power, but any other force, than the force of public opinion, exerted with coolness and firmness, so as

19

to bring the majority to see the general good, and to act so as to promote it. Governors may also see the dangers arising from a system of coercion and of power improperly exercised. But to attempt to bury the past in oblivion is a fruitless effort. History will record in a black page, the excesses and errors committed by both sides; and a lasting memorial that cannot be obliterated, while memory holds its place, is recorded in the recollection of thousands.[43]

Five years later, just after Emmet's insurrection, and the hanging and beheading of Thomas Russell in 1803, we have a brief glimpse of Hancock through the pages of the Drennan Letters. He was sitting alone in a coffee house reading, while those at the next table were discussing recent events. A priest was holding up the example of the doctor who informed on Thomas Russell for sacrificing private friendship for public good, when John Hancock lifted his eyes from the paper, and said "And would'st thee wish for such a friend?"[44] Hancock's question in a way gives a measure of the depth of the man.

Faith and practice

In Lambeg, the public were less familiar with Hancock the political radical, but John Hancock the man was well known to them. He had shown his concern and been practical in his efforts on their behalf in times of need. In 1800, a famine year,[45] the price of wheat in Mark Lane had risen to 130 shillings a quarter and the retail price of oatmeal to ten shillings the sieve of 20 lbs. John Hancock imported from Philadelphia 200 tons of Indian meal, the first time it was seen in Ulster. He also brought over 500 barrels of American flour and both were sold at cost price to distressed families in Lisburn.[46] His many charitable acts were not recorded but, in 1817, "when death and disease pressed heavily on Lisburn," he purchased, along with John Rogers, double-handed spinning wheels and opened a school to train women and girls in their use.[47] The purchase of their output was guaranteed, although the scheme failed as a commercial venture.

John Hancock died at Lisburn on 25 September 1823, aged 61, and in an act of reconciliation he was buried in the Friends' burial ground beside the Meeting House in Jackson's Lane, now Railway Street. His large funeral was reported in the *Commercial Chronicle* and the *Belfast News Letter*.

This very valuable man was buried on Sunday, in the Quaker's burying-ground in Lisburn. His remains were followed to the tomb by a large concourse of people of all denominations. The most respectable inhabitants of Lisburn and its vicinity assembled to pay their respect to a fellow townsman, whose solid and substantial qualities they had long admired. The poor with the sincerity, which generally characterizes them, followed the remains of their friend and protector. They called to their recollection those sad and calamitous days when nobody almost was to be found at the bedside of a dying victim to the typhus fever, but the inestimable individual whose loss they had to lament. Protestants, Presbyterians, and Catholics, felt it a duty they owed to this inflexible advocate of public justice, to pay him the last sad honours of the grave. When the body had arrived at its destined abode, Doctor Tennant, one of the most intimate and confidential friends of the deceased, addressed the surrounding multitude.[48]

We will refer to the work of John Hancock as a bleacher and linen draper at another time, but for the present we record the graveside tribute of his old friend Dr Robert Tennant.

> John Hancock had no formal creed, religious or political, but the fervent aspiration of his heart was – glory to God in the highest, on earth peace, and good will towards men: this he thought could never be attained without freedom – that freedom which becomes men possessing reason, and desirous of happiness; who should not only be free to secure that happiness, but encouraged and directed by freely chosen collective wisdom in the pursuit of it. This made him the ardent and zealous advocate of liberty, the uncompromising enemy of corruption in the State or Church, and of all tyranny or assumed power in either, inconsistent with the perfect exercise of individual exertion to procure a man's own good, and that of the society of which he is a member. Our late friend was a Reformer indeed … he went to the root of the matter both as to the external system and the internal qualifications, by which alone that system can be advanced to perfection; he would have man stand erect in freedom, that he might successfully cultivate their dispositions, which confer upon freedom all its value. To this end all his efforts were directed, his writing breathed the same spirit, and his precepts were powerfully recommended by his example. Indeed agreeable to his own doctrine, his life was a practical comment on moral and political science: he devoted himself to practical utility, and all his extraordinary powers were employed with an energy rarely witnessed, to do good, and to communicate good, to all within the sphere of his activity, without regard to differences of opinion, …[49]

We speak of a man of whom few will have heard and we are indebted to the scholarly research of Neville H Newhouse, former headmaster of Friends' School, who published his work on John Hancock in the journal of the *Royal Society of Antiquaries of Ireland,* 1971. Newhouse concludes his article by asking the question, "What is the judgement of posterity on such a man?" With the benefits of his research he answers the question: "Chiefly praise – he was so often on the side of the angels, and he sought so earnestly to unite faith and practice, to do what he preached. Most men in any age in history would have been glad of such a friend." [50]

Lambeg Road arch 1936.
SCC

McMurray, who owned the Bleach Green, so that he could close it down. It then served as a barber's shop, confectioners, a general store and Post Office. The building was listed in 1986.[96] The adjoining gateway led to what was known in the 1930s as Crothers' Loft, where local youths were taught boxing in an informal youth club. There was a proper boxing ring with all the equipment in the club, which was organised by Bob Brown, a gentleman from Cottage Row, one who you would not associate with boxing. In the past, a high stone wall with window openings in the upper level, having yellow brick surrounds, formed the boundary wall of an uncompleted building that ran parallel to the Lambeg Road, where Priory Close now stands. Jonathan Richardson of Lambeg House built the wall for a row of barns and sheds, but the work was halted in a dispute with the Richardsons of Glenmore and never completed. Stones from the demolished wall are now incorporated in the elevations of the bungalows in Priory Close.

A 1936 photograph (above) of an Orange arch erected over Lambeg Road at this point, shows clearly some of the buildings we have described. Crothers' shop in the left foreground abuts the stone wall with eight window-openings. On the right of the picture the two brick houses, three curved roofed barns projecting above the wall, and the Manager's house beyond, were the property of the Linen Research Institute. The street is clean and neat and the children are dressed in their best. The Arch was erected for the annual Twelfth of July Orange demonstration and the parade that year walked to the church field to mark the opening of the local Orange Hall by LOL 912, the first and only occasion that that venue was used. The arch was declared

Lambeg Presbyterian
Church Hall.

open by Miss Norah Richardson, Lambeg House.[97] Those present for the photograph
have been identified. To the left of the arch: E Turkington, unknown; under the arch
from left to right: May Rollins, Molly Hall, Olive Bruce, E Hillen, William Wright
(with Dick in his arms), Cecil Parker, Terry Law on the bicycle, John Mulholland,
Derick Law, Mrs Cunningham, Susan Cullen (with Jack Cullen) in front, Mrs
Crothers, who owned the shop, Maxwell Reid, John Herron, Malcolm Crangle,
Artie McDonald, Jim Thompson, Norman Hall with the dog; front row left to right:
William Press, Walter Mulholland, Jack McMullan and Norman Mulholland.

Further down the street a housing development, called Priory Close, a small estate,
which has achieved numerous awards for its high standards, led to the dispatch
of Lambeg Presbyterian Church Hall, where the Harmony Hill congregation can
trace its roots back to a Sunday school, established there in 1902 by First Lisburn
Presbyterian Church. During the war, the church hall was used as an army billet and
the Sunday School was temporarily located in McDonnell's shed near the railway
bridge. This temporary location also doubled as accommodation for some evacuees
from Belfast during the Blitz. The Irish Order of Good Templars, a temperance
organisation with several lodges in Lisburn, held dances and concerts in a hall
adjacent to the church hall. These were well attended by the local people and the
concert programmes were organised on a 'Sing, Say or Pay' basis. The anonymous
nineteenth-century poem, *Papa's Letter*, is from the repertoire of Martha Moore, who
was a regular attendee at these concerts. The Moore family were not known for their
musical ability and, as they couldn't afford to pay, they said recitations.

Martha Moore.

PAPA'S LETTER

I was sitting in my study,
Writing letters when I heard
"Please dear Mama, Mary told me
Mama mustn't be disturbed."

"But I's tired of the kitty;
Want some ozzer fing to do.
Writing letters, is ou Mama?
Tan't I write a letter too?"

"Not now, darling, Mama's busy;
Run and play with kitty, now."
"No, no Mama, me write letter;
Tan, if 'ou will show me how."

I would paint my darling's portrait
As his sweet eyes searched my face.
Hair of gold, eyes of azure,
Form of childish, witching grace.

But the eager face was clouded,
As I slowly shook my head,
Till I said: "I'll make a letter
Of you, darling boy, instead."

So I parted back the tresses
From his forehead high and white,
And a stamp in sport I pasted
'Mid its waves of golden light.

Then I said, "Now little letter,
Go away and bear good news."
And I smiled as down the staircase
Clattered loud the little shoes.

Down the street the baby hastened
Till he reached the office door.
"I'se a letter, Mr Postman;
Is there room for any more?

'Cause this letter's going to Papa,
Papa lives with God 'ou know,
Mama sent me for a letter,
Do 'ou fink at I tan go?"

CHAPTER 2
The Church Walk

We step out now on the old road for Belfast, via Malone, and follow the footpath for about three-quarters of a mile along the boundary of Aberdelghy, to Lambeg Parish Church and the Wolfenden's Bridge. To keep us company along the way, allow me to introduce you to James McKowen, the Bard of Lambeg, who probably walked this way on his visits to the theatre in Belfast.[1] We can imagine him composing verses in his head as he strode along, perhaps for his popular song *The Ould Irish Jig:*

> I've heard how our jig came in fashion –
> And believe that the story is true –
> By Adam and Eve 'twas invented,
> The reason was, partners were few.
> And, though they could both dance the polka,
> Eve thought it was not over-chaste;
> She preferred our ould jig to be dancing –
> And faith, I approve of her taste.

James McKowen was born in Lambeg in 1814 and attended school for a short period. He started work in Barbour's Thread mills at Hilden and then moved to Glenmore bleach works, where he was employed for the next forty years, and in his retirement he was granted a small pension. His mother's keen literary tastes may have influenced him, for Mrs McKowen was the former Miss Johnson, daughter of John Johnson, who kept an inn in Bow Street, Lisburn. There was an improvised theatre at the rear of the inn, where the players in Robert Owenson's acting company performed and Miss Johnson spent many evenings with Robert Owenson and his daughters, Sydney and Olivia. Olivia later became Lady Olivia Clarke and published a comedy entitled *The Irishwoman*. Her older sister Sydney, later the famous writer and patriot Lady Morgan, moved in literary and social circles in both Dublin and London as an established writer of novels, essays and travel books. Her novels, which included *The Wild Irish Girl, O'Donnel, Florence Macarthy* and *O'Briens and the O'Flahertys*, were considered important in their time. Another member of Robert Owenson's troupe was Miss Elizabeth O'Neill, the fifteen-year-old leading lady, who later became Lady Becher.

Mrs McKowen may have encouraged her son's taste for the theatre, but James was also an avid reader and included Shakespeare, Scott, Burns, Byron and Moore among his favourites. In a letter to a publisher, in which he questions the price charged, or indeed overcharged, for a pamphlet of poems by another poet, he compares it to the cost of a Bible and gives us his personal appreciation of the poetry of the Bible.

> My it was only the other day that a man came into my house to sell Bibles, and from this man I bought a Bible, 'bound in Morocco', so they say, having 'marginal references' and a very pretty representation of a lion and unicorn on the title page, for eighteen pence! And yet this book; this eighteenpenny Bible, contains the glorious poetry of Isaiah and of David, and contains also that greatest and grandest of all poems ever produced or written, the Book of Job.[2]

McKowen's appetite for reading material covered a wide range of authors and for many years he searched for the works of Bishop Jeremy Taylor, and wrote "but neither among my friends, nor in the library of the Dunmurry Reading Society[3] nor in that of the Belfast working classes were they to be found …" In the same letter to Alexander Orr, Minister of Lambeg, written in 1857, he asks to borrow Taylor's works one volume at a time and compares Dean Swift with Bishop Taylor, criticizes the local clergy and supports building conservation, all in the space of one paragraph.

> For a few shillings one may purchase the works of that wit, misanthrope and I fear I may add, madman, Swift, while those of Bishop Taylor are not to be obtained for less than a good round sum of money. And yet there is not more difference between the magnificent magnolia and the 'rough burr thistle' than there is between Taylor and Swift … It does not speak well for the 'spread of education' that Taylor's works are still so scarce and so expensive – nor do I think it redounds much to the credit of the Clergy of this Diocese, that 'Magheralave House', in which tradition says Taylor sometimes resided, is almost a ruin.[4]

McKowen never published a volume of his own verse but contributed to the *Nation* under the *nom de plume* Curlew, and in other publications he was known as Kitty

Conner. He exchanged verses with many of the working class, agricultural and handloom weaving poets of the day, such as David Herbison and Francis Davis, the 'Belfast Man'. His note to Ralph Varian, the anthologist, which stated, "there is a kind of Scotch dialect spoken in these parts of Co Antrim" is in contrast to the politically induced Ulster Scots revival of this century with its emphasis on a 'language'. It has been said of McKowen that "few men enjoyed life with greater zeal than he did; he made many friends for himself, and his genial countenance and happy disposition never failed in imparting to others a share of his joyous temperament." [5]

We have arrived at Lambeg Parish Church where we will part company with him for this was James McKowen's journeys end in 1889; he is buried in the churchyard here in a family grave.[6] Cross the road with care and turn up the drive to the church. We will have call to use McKowen's verse on other occasions but a few lines of praise written by his friend David Herbison of Dunclug in November 1869 will serve as his epitaph.

The Bard of Lambeg

I remember it well
When I heard his first song
How the echoing dell
Bore its music along.
All nature was glad
Nought of care could be seen
While that sweet song we had –
Lovely Kate of Glenkeen.

LAMBEG PARISH CHURCH

It is generally accepted that the church of Lambeg is situated on the site of an earlier monastic settlement. In Lewis' *Topographical Dictionary of Ireland* (1837) we read, "Lambeg church occupies the site of an ancient monastery said to have been founded in the fifteenth century by MacDonnell for Franciscan friars of the third order" and support for this statement is found in a State Paper of 1601 and Archdalls' *Monasticon Hibernicum* published in 1722.[7] The *Ordnance Survey Memoirs* refer to a local tradition that the graveyard was the site of an ancient nunnery as well as a church. The walled foundations of the nunnery have often been exposed when graves were opened on the site and a low portion of ground is known as the Nun's Garden. Monastery or nunnery? We can accommodate both if we accept another old tradition, referred to by HC Marshall, that there were two religious houses, one on the south side of the church and the other across the river on the former site of Lambeg Bleaching, Dyeing and Finishing Company. Marshall supports this belief by quoting an extract from a notebook belonging to the Rev Edward Cupples, and written in 1806, which states that the nunnery was connected to the monastery

Lambeg Parish Church.

by a subterranean passage under the River Lagan. Nothing is ever straightforward, however, and Cupples places the monastery beside the church, where you thought the nunnery was, but introduces a secret tunnel for added value.[8]

Lambeg church is clearly marked on a map of Ulster dated 1598, which is now in the British Museum. This is the earliest date for which there is proof of a church on this site. By 1657 the church was in a ruined condition according to an Inquisition taken in Antrim in that year. In 1657 the Parish of Lambeg was amalgamated with that of Blaris and the rectors of Lisburn were responsible for the services in Lambeg, and all the other work of the Parish up to 1737, when a new church was built. This church, the tower of which is the only part that remains today, was said to have been built by the Wolfenden family, who lived at what is now Chrome Hill. In 1737 the tower was surmounted by a square, wooden cupola tapering to a height of twenty feet at the top, on which was a weathercock. In 1824 the church was enlarged and then in 1849, under the guidance of the Rev Alexander Orr, it was completely rebuilt, with the exception of the tower. The south aisle of the church was altered in 1870 to increase the seating capacity to 480 persons. Renovations, modernisation and improvements have continued over the past century supported by the congregation, which today comprises some 450 families.

The Roll of Honour on the War Memorial in the church contains the names of twenty men from the Parish of Lambeg who made the supreme sacrifice in the Great War, among them local man Rifleman Robert Daniel Mc Cabe, 18196, who served with the 11th Battalion, Royal Irish Rifles and died at the Lisburn Infirmary on 11 October 1917, from injuries received on active service, aged twenty-seven. He suffered from the effects of gas-poisoning and internal injuries and was discharged from military service about ten days before his death. Rifleman McCabe was one of four brothers who joined the army; two others were also discharged.[9] His parents, Henry and Jean McCabe, lived at Green Hill. He was buried with full military honours at Lambeg with a salute fired at the graveside. South of the west end of the church you will find the Commonwealth War Grave Memorial, where he is remembered with honour.

McCabe Memorial.

The churchyard is full of interest and if you take time to explore you will find stones inscribed with the names of those that we encounter on our journey and others associated with the history of the Lisburn area; Wolfenden, Gordon, Niven, Dubourdieu, Boomer, Barbour, Williamson and Richardson. An interesting grave is that of Essy Pelan, which has a tragic love story attached to it. Essy's lover emigrated to America with the intention of making his fortune so that he could return and share his life with her. While he was in America, a rumour reached Essy that he had transferred his affection to someone else. Essy believed this story, which was completely untrue.[10] When her lover returned, he found that Essy had died of a broken heart and had been buried in Lambeg churchyard in her bridal dress, while her bridal wreath, according to tradition, was laid on her grave. Essy Pelan died on the anniversary of her birthday, 1 March 1833, aged twenty-one years. The gravestone is in the form of a broken column on a rectangular base, with the following inscriptions:

Separated below but united above.
For love is strong as death. Solomon's Song, 8:6.

in the western Mediterranean at latitude 42° 15' N longitude 4° 09' E; children Gorg, Lenord and Dorethy of Gorg Bullmer; and a memorial erected to the youthful Mary Wright by the operatives of Lambeg Weaving Factory. Any questions?

As we prepare to take our leave of the good souls who are at permanent rest here, marked out and mourned by ageing stones, we should spare a thought for those who may have left their plot much sooner than they

Lambeg PE School, 1933.
SCC

expected – courtesy of the resurrectionists! During the nineteenth century, the need for surgical training in schools of anatomy, particularly in Glasgow and Edinburgh, fuelled a market for cadavers, which was supplied from churchyards in Scotland and by imports from Ireland. It was suspected that Lambeg had its own *Burke and Hare*[23] character in the person of James Dickson, the Sexton, who, according to the Vestry record for 20 December 1830, was dismissed "in consequence of its being suspected that he aided in raising some dead bodies which were ascertained to have been carried away from the churchyard."[24]

As we leave the church grounds we are aware that two avenues lead to the church. The original avenue provided by the Richardson family for the use of coaches was not wide enough for the Barbour family car so they arranged for a new avenue to be constructed in 1924. The lime trees, which we pass below, were not planted till 1943. On our way out, we notice an inappropriate rustic brick toilet block in the car park, which marks the site of the former schoolhouse. The materials from the old church were used to erect a one-room school in 1849, called Lambeg Village Schoolhouse,

Lambeg village schoolhouse.
SCC

which replaced an old school at Ballyskeagh.[25] It was built on land which was the property of Jonathan Richardson of Lambeg House and, about 1896, ownership passed to Mr John M Milligen and then to Mr WR McMurray. Once a year, Mr John M Milliken came down to the school to examine all the children and award prizes. The school was governed by the Church Education Society from 1849 to 1892, when it was placed under the National Board and in 1928 it transferred to the Ministry of Education for Northern Ireland. The Parish used it until it was demolished in 1954.

Wolfenden's Bridge.

WOLFENDEN'S BRIDGE

Wolfenden's Bridge over the River Lagan is difficult to appreciate while driving a car, but it looks most impressive with its nine spans, when viewed from the river and a good view can be obtained from the church car park. The bridge, which links Counties Antrim and Down, is built of basalt and sandstone rubble, with triangular cutwaters both upstream and downstream. Five of the arches span the river and the remaining four are flood arches on the Co Down side. Thomas Fagan of the Ordnance Survey, in the autumn of 1837, wrote: "that bridge across the Lagan a short distance north of the village of Lambeg and locally called Wolfenden's bridge, has nine half-circle arches; span of each arch fifteen feet, breadth of the road on the bridge eighteen feet; average height of parapets 2ft 6in, thickness of parapets 1ft 4in; length of the bridge fifty-two yards, length of the parapets on either side of the road 120 yards. The bridge and parapets are built of whinstone and seem in permanent condition at present. It is said to be a very old bridge." [26] The Lagan is a fordable river above Belfast, but in the past there were regular fords at fixed points. The most important of these was the one at Belfast, another where the first lock on the canal was, this one near Lambeg and another at Moira.[27]

CHAPTER 3
Chrome Hill and Lambeg Mills

We proceed to cross the Wolfenden's Bridge, making sure to remain on the pavement, for this section of our walk is very dangerous for pedestrians, and you must exercise extreme caution. In front of us to the right, on the Co Down side of the river, hidden among the trees, sits Chrome Hill, a secluded house of great character. The original small farm dwelling, out of which the house has grown, was probably built some time in the second half of the seventeenth century and Abraham Wolfenden, who gave shelter here to King William on his way to the Boyne in 1690, is the earliest known occupant.[1] The house was at various times called Harmony Hill and Lambeg House.[2] Sir Charles Brett writes: "the present exterior appearance, a five-bay two-storey white-painted roughcast house with lower extension on the right and taller extension to the left, is mostly of the early 1830s, when Richard Niven bought the Lambeg works … he changed the name of the house, formerly known as Lambeg House, to Chrome Hill." [3] A copy of Benn's, *The History of the Town of Belfast*, which is inscribed Richd Niven, Chrome Hill, 15 Aug 1823, indicates an earlier date for him being in residence.[4] Samuel Lewis in his *Topographical Dictionary*, 1837, writes "Chrome Hill, also a spacious modern mansion, was erected by R Niven Esq, late of Manchester, who established here some extensive works for printing muslin, in which he first applied with success his invention of the 'Ba Chrome', now universally used … from which circumstance he named his estate".[5]

Niven inserted his own coat of arms into the pediment above the front door when he bought the house and carried out some alterations and improvements.

Chrome Hill.
ILC & LM

Richard Niven Jnr (1839–1914).
ILC & LM

He died in 1866, and is buried in the Parish churchyard in a grave surrounded by an iron railing. His son, Richard Niven Jnr (1839–1914), formerly of Chrome Hill, and afterwards of Marlborough Park, Belfast, died at Brighton in 1914.[6] A member of the firm of Richardson & Niven, linen manufacturers, he was a man of taste and culture; an artist in both watercolour and oil, with an abiding interest in literature. An enthusiastic Orangeman and historian, his publications varied from *Orangeism as it was and is*; *A concise history of the rise and progress of the Institution*, to the light hearted and humorous volumes; *On the road to the Boyne* and *The life of St Patrick*.[7] His widowed mother continued to live in the house until her death in 1899. It was then purchased by John M Milligan, a coal merchant who made some changes and lived there for about three years before moving to Glenmore in 1901. It was rented out to a Major Adam P Jenkins and then to Benjamin C Hobson of Ravarnet Mill.[8] In 1921 Milligan sold the place to a Mr FG Barrett, who used it as the setting for the wedding of his daughter to a Mr McCausland, a seed merchant from Blaris.[9] In 1924 the Downer family purchased it and Mrs Margaret Josephine Downer lived there until her death in 1967, when Robert McKinstry, the architect, acquired it. In 2004 the house was purchased by its present owner, Dawson Stelfox, also an architect and the first Irishman to conquer Everest.

ROBERT GEMMILL

The extent of the Wolfenden's involvement in the cotton industry is not recorded but there is information on Robert Gemmill, a native of Scotland, who established a cotton factory here at the beginning of the nineteenth century.[36] Hugh McCall, in his summary of cotton mills in Belfast and its neighbourhood, lists Robert Gemmill of Lambeg, erecting a mill in 1810, and employing 200 hands, with fifty horsepower of machinery.[37] The cotton was not only spun, but also manufactured into muslin and calico, and afterwards bleached and finished for the market, so that the whole process of the cotton trade was carried out to high standards.[38] In 1823 the business was said to provide employment and support for 500 people producing muslins and calicoes for the home market, with occasional exports to America and the West Indies. Spun cotton yarn from this manufacturer was exported to Russia through their Glasgow agents.[39] The large numbers of operatives employed by the business was due, in part, to what was known as the 'putting out' system, which was implemented on an extensive scale by the cotton industry in the 1780s.[40] The manufacturers provided yarn to the weavers enabling them to weave at home and when they brought back the finished web they were paid for weaving it. The manufacturer was 'putting out' the work to be done by the weaver, but on his terms and conditions, having provided the yarn.

In addition to the Lambeg enterprise Robert Gemmill was in partnership, as a bleacher, with Samuel Waring at Collin, where they traded as Gemmill & Waring. That partnership was dissolved by mutual consent in August 1812, but Gemmill determined to continue on his own account at the same place where he hoped "by an unremitting attention to the bleaching and finishing of every description of cotton goods, to merit a continuance of that liberal share of public favour so amply experienced by the late firm".[41] Later that year, he advertised the sale of an 18 feet diameter overshot water wheel, less than three years old, and placed a recruitment notice for two experienced loft men.[42]

Obtaining skilled and experienced labour seems to have been an ongoing problem. Back in 1806, in a letter to McConnel & Kennedy, the Manchester cotton-spinning company, Gemmill complained about the labour situation in Ireland, claiming there were so many small manufacturers in the country that "I cannot get good weavers to work the work I wish, being 100 weavers short of my employment".[43] Judging from an advertisement in the *Belfast News Letter* in 1814, labour shortages continued to contribute to his difficulties.[44]

> Wanted at Lambeg Cotton Mill, near Lisburn, Throstle and Mule Spinners; also Card Room Workers, to whom liberal wages will be given.

Eighteen months later, in September 1815, the workers in Lambeg were laid off, and the house, farm, factory and machinery were advertised for sale in the *Belfast News Letter*.[45]

> Lambeg Cotton Factory, muslin bleach green houses and land to be sold. Most conveniently and pleasantly situated on the great north road leading from Belfast to Dublin only five miles from the former and two miles from Lisburn. The dwelling house is roomy and commodious and in thorough repair with large gardens attached well-enclosed and extensive office houses all in good order. The farm contains 32 acres English of excellent lands in good heart in which are twelve houses for workers all convenient to the works (most of which are still inhabited by the workers lately employed). The cotton factory and bleach green are not to be surpassed in point of situation in the north of Ireland and are constantly supplied with water from the River Lagan and canal and not a furlong from the latter in the heart of a manufacturing country. The machinery of the factory consists of 1224 Throstle and 912 Mule spindles with all necessary preparation in complete working order a Smith's forge Turners shop. The wheel is 13ft diameter, by 10ft in the bucket. The bleach green is in good repair and is constantly supplied with best spring water.

The business relationship, if any, between the Gemmills and the Wolfenden family is uncertain. In 1824, "Richard Wolfenden, junior and senior", presumably father and son, placed an advertisement for a person to manufacture calico on commission. The 1815 notice for the sale of the cotton factory invited interested parties to apply to Richard Wolfenden, a strong indication of a financial interest of that party in the sale of the property, which was held under a lease from the Marquis of Hertford. The Hertford estate records show Robert Gemmill in possession of the fifty acres of land, comprising the factory site and the residence at Chrome Hill, which later transferred to Mr Nevin.[46] It is not possible to say with certainty that the Gemmills took up residence at Chrome Hill, but it is recorded that Samuel Gemmill, a muslin and calico bleacher, was based in Lambeg in 1819 [47] and was a churchwarden in the Parish church in 1820.[48] Robert Gemmill's address is always recorded as Donegall Street, Belfast. In the records of the Belfast Academical Institution Robert Gemmill is named as a subscriber and John and Robert Gemmill are listed in the 1816 roll books as scholars, with their father listed as Robert Gemmill of Donegall Street, Belfast.[49] In 1819 Robert Gemmill Jnr "from Lambeg, near Belfast" is listed as a scholar, a positive indicator that the family were living at Chrome Hill.[50]

In the depression, which followed the end of the Napoleonic war, the cotton manufacturers reduced wages in an attempt to lower production costs and a bitter conflict with the weavers ensued. By 1811 a cotton operatives union was in existence in the United Kingdom and the weavers in Belfast and Lisburn were organised and in militant mood. In April 1815 a great number of cotton weavers from the Maze marched through Lambeg to Belfast and left their unfinished webs at the offices of the different manufacturers, in protest at the reduced wages.[51] Rioting broke out when an attempt was made to arrest the leaders. In March 1816 a party of men attempted to blow up the home of an unpopular muslin manufacturer, Mr Francis Johnson, in Peters-hill, Belfast, when he and his family were asleep.[52] Two young weavers, John Magill and John Doe, were arrested and hanged in High Street, Belfast, in September for taking part in the attack.[53] In April 1817, Gordon Maxwell, the Lisburn President of the Muslin Weavers' Society was shot and fatally wounded on the Malone Road.[54] He accused his employer, John McCann, of involvement before he died. McCann was put on trial but acquitted. In 1818 there was another major strike. Conditions were difficult throughout the industry.

By January 1820 Robert Gemmill of Lambeg was bankrupt and a notice placed in the *Belfast News Letter* by the assignee was directed to those weavers employed by Gemmill on the putting out system:

> In the matter of Robert Gemill of Lambeg a bankrupt. All weavers who have drawn work from the office of the said bankrupt are hereby noticed without fail to return it when wove, to No 66 Ann St. The accounts of any work not returned in one month from this date will be handed over to their securities on payment. Those indebted to the estate, will please have their accounts settled immediately with John Baine assignee. Belfast 11 January 1820.[55]

The Gemmills at Lambeg, whether Robert or Samuel, were survivors in business terms; the relationship between them is unclear. Samuel Gemmill remained in business for several more years. He appears in the Belfast section of *Piggotts Directory*, 1824, as "Saml. Gemmell, Lambeg, a calico printer" and in the Lisburn section of the same directory, Gemil & McPherson are listed as calico printers and cotton spinners.[56] Market conditions were difficult. In Belfast and its neighbourhood, a strike, or lock out, at the start of 1826 affected all the cotton mills and a resolution in April by the proprietors to re-open, "with other hands than those that left their employment," was signed by Robert Gemmill among others.[57] Robert Gemmill was still connected to Lambeg print works in 1826, according to a death notice for Mr Robert Jones, a tradesman originally from Blakely, Manchester, who died there in 1826.[58] Robert Gemmill seems to have died some time before 1828 and in March 1830 an auction of all the cotton spinning machinery was advertised to take place on the premises, at Lambeg Print Works.[59] This is the last record of Lambeg as a cotton-spinning base; various manufacturers subsequently used the buildings, partly as a printing works, bleach works, beetling works and a bleaching, dyeing, and finishing works.

RICHARD NIVEN

Richard Niven, who came from Manchester, settled at Chrome Hill and purchased the Lambeg works. In Manchester he had been in partnership with Andreas Kurtz (1781–1846), a chemist, who loved his science and revelled in research. They commenced a manufacturing works in Liverpool to manufacture bi-chromate of potash, colours and dyes. John Fenwick Allen, in his 1906 profile of Kurtz, writes,

> This partnership, as long as it lasted, was most fortunate, and a very successful and lucrative business was carried on. Kurtz proved himself to be a most skilful, practical chemist and competent manufacturer, whilst Niven was an excellent man of business, who discovered markets and customers for their products, and was a clever salesman. About the year 1828 fortune smiled upon them so graciously that in one year they made a profit, which in those days was looked upon as a very handsome fortune. Whether there were faults on both sides we cannot now relate; but Kurtz was naturally excitable, irritable and hasty, and although the relationship between Niven and himself had contributed so largely to the benefit of both, they nevertheless quarrelled, and the partnership was dissolved. To Kurtz this event was little short of a calamity. Niven was the very man he needed to be associated with. Kurtz was no man of business, although a good arithmetician and fair mathematician his tastes drove him to his laboratory instead of his counting house; chemical experiments were far more congenial to him than the keeping of accounts, and the superintendence of the processes of manufacture than the visiting of markets, the winning of customers and the disposal of goods.[60]

Richard Niven was to demonstrate his entrepreneurial skills, on arriving at Lambeg, by successfully establishing extensive printworks where he produced coloured muslins by applying bichromates to fix the colours.[61] From the outset he gave employment to over fifty block printers and had two machines in constant operation. By 1835 Niven had seventy block tables and two machines.[62] The first edition of the Ordnance Survey map in 1834 shows the calico print works and Chrome Hill. The works were extensive with two printing houses, three factory buildings, colour house, furnace and boiler house, bleach house and blue house. In 1838 operations ceased, the print works was converted into a muslin bleach green and the calico printing machinery, printing-tables, blocks, colours and equipment were sold without reserve, at auction.[63] Samuel Lewis, writing in 1837, also claims for Mr Niven the introduction of oxide of chrome into the ornamental departments of the 'China manufacture'.[64] Niven would have been knowledgeable on this subject, his former partner Kurtz was known to have experimented with glazes for earthenware, but there is no evidence of a china manufacture having been established at Lambeg at this period.[65] We mention, in passing, John Dubourdieu's reference, to "a very ancient establishment" of a Pottery at Lambeg, which was confined to the courser wares and never made any

Andreas Kurtz. (1781–1846).

Card-cutting room in the Lambeg Weaving Company's factory, 1926. The worker in the centre is preparing the cards by punching, the other two operatives are working on card-copying machines.

EHS

Lambeg Weaving Co Ltd.

SCC

improvement.[66] It was established at the end of the seventeenth century by a family of English settlers.[67]

McAdam's list of bleachers states that McConkey & Howie, bleachers at Lambeg, were operating in 1839 on an extensive scale and bleaching about 15,000 pieces per annum. *Henderson's Directory* lists them as operating there in 1844 at a time when, according to Samuel Lewis, Richard Niven was also at Lambeg.[68] He may still have had part of the works that were formerly used for printing. In 1844 Jonathan Richardson required beetling engines to finish bleached cloth and rented the dye works from Richard Niven for twenty-one years, renewed for a further forty years. There was a demand for linen after the American Civil War and, about 1866, Richard Niven Jnr joined in a partnership with John and Alexander Richardson to build a weaving factory alongside the dye works, which contained 200 plain looms.[69] Alexander Airth Richardson was head of the firm, which traded as Richardson & Niven.[70] A major fire in 1883 almost completely destroyed the weaving factory, which was rebuilt, but on a smaller scale.[71] John Richardson withdrew from the partnership in 1892 and the weaving factory and dye works were incorporated into a limited company, which was wound up in 1900.[72]

THE 1900s

In 1900 Messrs Glendinning, McLeish & Co Ltd of Belfast, purchased the factory and dye works and gradually converted all the looms to weave damask and enlarged

Church Hill, Lambeg.

the factory to double its original size.[73] In the 1930s the factory contained 320 looms and employed about 250 workers and the fine damask tablecloths, napkins and towels, which they produced, had a worldwide reputation.[74] Thirty-eight worker's houses were built at Ballyskeagh at a cost of £6,000.[75] The dye works were rented to Messrs Gee, Samuels and Dougan in 1901, but Samuels and Dugan withdrew from the business in 1908 and Mr Gee, in association with Glendinning, McLeish & Co, established a private limited company, which employed about forty operatives, and traded as The Factory Dye Works Ltd.[76] Mr Gee's son, Dr Brian Cameron Gee, managed the dye works in the late 1930s but gave up the post in 1942, when the industry contracted due to wartime conditions. He then worked as a research chemist in the Linen Industry Research Association, but resigned in 1947, when he was appointed lecturer in charge of the bleaching and dyeing section of the College of Technology, Belfast. Dr Gee was appointed Principal of Portadown Technical School in 1953. During World War II, when Short and Harland dispersed their aircraft manufacturing operations to prevent air attacks, the weaving factory was converted

Letterhead – Lambeg
Weaving Co Ltd, 1957.

for the manufacture of tail planes, flaps, fins and rudders.[77] A similar operation at Altona, Lisburn, manufactured fuselage sections.[78] The Lambeg Weaving Co Ltd closed in 1958 with a loss of 200 jobs.

Lambeg Mills is still a location for industry. Alexander Boyd Displays, a design and printing company, and Gregg & Patterson, structural steel fabricators and erectors, occupy the site.

There is nothing to merit a visit to the Mills, so we will now retrace our steps back over the Wolfenden's Bridge, up Church Hill and return to the village. On this side of the bridge, we notice a terrace of mill houses with two date stones built into the front elevation, bearing dates 1718 and 1903, with initials A W J and JMM respectively. The terrace originally comprised single storey thatched cottages, which were rebuilt as two storey houses following a fire in 1903. Could the initials, which accompany the original date of 1718, signify A and J Wolfenden, and those with the 1903 date, John M Milligan? The house at the end of the terrace incorporated a weaver's workshop. On the other side of the bridge an attractive terrace of mill houses leads the approach to Church Hill.

Demolition of the Lambeg
Weaving Company's
150 foot factory chimney,
8 March 1961.
BNL

CHAPTER 5

Towards Tullynacross

L̲ambeg Bridge was built of whinstone, with three main arches over the river and three dry arches on the Down side, which were necessary in case of high floods.[1] The arches spanning the river had a twenty-one foot span and the dry arches had a seven foot span. Remember to use the adjoining footbridge provided for your safety.

Immediately after crossing the bridge, turn right along the tow-path and travel for a short distance towards Hilden. We are now in the Co Down, on land that was originally part of the Glenmore House demesne. The house is no longer visible through the trees to our right but the splendour of the original site, and the mature trees in the parkland, are captured in Joseph Molloy's [2] view (overleaf), engraved by Edward K Proctor in 1832.[3] About the same time, the Lisburn lawyer, Henry Bayly, published a poem on Lisburn which included a description of 'Williamson's domain', or Lambeg House as Glenmore was called at that time, when it was occupied by Robert Williamson.

Lambeg bridge.

I'm now away to Williamson's domain,
Where Nature's beauties rise in stately train;
Where groves in majesty expanding wide,
Rejoice in all the strength of Eastern pride;
And call the wearied Bard to catch the gale,
That breathes in honey through the elmy vale;
Where yonder spacious lawn its verdure shows –

See beauteous plantings Lambeg house inclose;
Trees in their gayest foliage ever green,
Are here on banks of crystal rivers seen;
And fairest fruits, whose healthful fragrance fills
The Zephyrs breathing o'er an hundred hills.[4]

Lambeg House, the seat of Robert Williamson Esq. Drawn by Joseph Molloy, engraved by Edward K Proctor, 1832.

Reproduced with the permission of the Linen Hall Library

GLENMORE BLEACH WORKS

A quarter of a mile upstream from the house lay Glenmore Bleach Works with its extensive bleach greens and mill ponds. We normally associate this bleach works with the Richardson name, but one must delve even further back into the history of bleaching to uncover the origin of the site as a bleach green. In Lendrick's map (1780)[5], four bleach greens are marked at Glenmore, all close to the Lagan and on the Co Antrim side. Lendrick names them as Mr Hancock, Mr Hunter, Mr Delacherois and Edward Hogg. The Hancock green was sold to the Richardsons about 1830. The Hunters, who are recorded as owners of the bleach green in 1780, sold to the

Left: Glenmore bleachworks with linen on the grass; the Deadwall Plantation in the foreground with Hilden village, Glenmore Cottage, Grafton Crescent and Hilden School in the distance.

© English Heritage

Below: The spread fields at Glenmore bleachworks. Glenmore Cottage in the foreground with Clonmore house and gate lodge in the distance.

© English Heritage

Richardsons sometime prior to 1800 and on a map dated 1819, belonging to Messrs Richardson, Sons & Owden, the Hunter site was marked 'JJ & J Richardson's green'.[6] The same map showed Delacherois' green as Mr Ward,[7] probably the Mr Ward who about that date purchased the damask factory of William Coulson of Lisburn. The 1819 map did not extend as far as the Hogg's bleach green.[8] The Hoggs remained there until about 1823, when William Hogg retired from the trade. Eventually the date stone on the front elevation records "Lambeg National School, 1849". The schoolhouse was sold by the church in 2000 and has recently been sympathetically converted to two residential properties, one of which retains an internal plaque inscribed, "Parish of Lambeg, Tullynacross Hall, Rev KA McReynolds Dip. Th." KA McReynolds has been Rector of Lambeg since 1989.

THOMAS CAMPBELL

A former Tullynacross scholar from an earlier era was Thomas Campbell, a minor local poet, who attended the school when Mr Richardson was the headmaster. Campbell was born in Sandy Row in 1855. Two years later the family moved to Derriaghy and lived there for five years before moving to the Low Road in 1862, where Thomas spent much of his life. Thomas Campbell worked for over fifty years in Hilden Mill (which we will look at shortly), having started there at the age of eleven. In 1884 Campbell issued a book of verse, *Lays From Lisnagarvey*, and in the preface he refers to the difficulties he had to contend with when writing – "They were composed by a mill operative in his leisure moments, who, from boyhood, has been nurtured among the whirl of belts and the din of machinery, – no enviable situation for the cultivation of the Muses." [39] A poem entitled *Reflections from a Window in Hilden Spinning Mill* refers to his days at Tullynacross and we can share this memory of his youth, as he looks towards us.

> Away to the left stands the old school-house yonder,
> Half surrounded and shaded by tall poplars grey,
> The playground of which, in those days, I was fonder
> Than the lessons the master required each day.
> Ah! often 'tis thus in the dawn of life's morning,
> By amusement and pleasure youth's oft led astray,
> The teaching of elders gives but feeble warning
> Of the end, while excitement has absolute sway. [40]

Thomas Campbell left Tullynacross and completed his schooling with Mr Samuel Hull at the Market Square Presbyterian Church School, Lisburn. When still a young man, he was involved in the setting up of the Lisburn Co-operative Society Ltd and was closely identified with the struggle of the Society at the beginning and its early prosperity. He served on the committee of the Society for twenty-five years. He was its first treasurer, and the President from 1892 to 1899. He had an interest in the Orange Institution and Freemasonry and these, together with his poetry, filled his leisure time. [41]

Thomas Campbell joined Saint Patrick's Masonic Lodge in Derriaghy in 1876 and was associated with numerous other lodges in the district. It is from a Masonic class of instruction held in Castle Street, Lisburn, and led by Campbell, that the formation of The Thomas Campbell Memorial Masonic Lodge, can be traced.[42] The lodge was constituted in November 1922 with warrant No 489, but contrary to the wishes of the members, the rules would not permit the lodge to be named after Thomas Campbell during his lifetime. Thomas Campbell was the first Worshipful Master and the lodge minute book contains his poem entitled *Faith, Hope and Charity*, which he read to members on the opening night.[43] We give the last verse.

Thus in Faith and Hope and Love
The Mason's footsteps guide
To that blest home that is above
Where peace and joy abide,
When there at last, a place we own,
And earthly cares resign
We'll meet around, The Great White Throne
As four, eight, nine.

Thomas Campbell was presented in February 1922 with an illuminated address on the occasion of his departure for Philadelphia to be with his family, but he did not have long to enjoy the reunion, for later that year, in November, the minutes of the Lodge record his death. In March 1923 the full name of the lodge was approved and from that date until now, the lodge has been known as The Thomas Campbell Memorial Lodge, No 489, Lisburn. Many of Campbell's poems, such as *Derriaghy* and *Address to an MM Apron* dealt with Masonic subjects. A large number of his poems appeared in the columns of the *Lisburn Standard* between 1884 and 1900; some under the anagrammatic *nom-de-guerre* of Pat McBlashmole, and others under the initials 'TC'.[44] Thomas Campbell is one of many scholars whose entry into the university of life began at Tullynacross.

Tullynacross pump.

TULLYNACROSS READING AND RECREATION ROOM

Next to the schoolhouse stood the Tullynacross Reading and Recreation Rooms, erected for the use of the workingmen of Tullynacross in 1896. Mr J Milne Barbour officially opened the rooms on the evening of Tuesday 29 December. He congratulated those present on the fine building they had secured and hoped it would be prized and used by them. The opening ceremony was reported in the *Northern Whig*. Mr Barbour was of the opinion that workingmen should be thoroughly conversant with the news and politics of the day, as well as with the great social and industrial problems dealt with in the daily papers. Magazines and periodicals would be provided and when members tired of reading they could spend an hour very profitably in the adjoining room, in a quiet chat and interesting games.

The Rev Benjamin Banks, Rector of Lambeg, gave as a motto for the working of the club the three words, Fairplay, Firmness and Fraternity, and hoped that nothing but the best of good nature would characterize the members dealings with one another. Henry Frazer, who was at that time the Principal of Tullynacross School, but later entered the church and became Vicar of St Peter's, Everton, Liverpool, in 1906, gave an account of how he had raised money and support to get the building erected. Mr Charles H Richardson, of Richardson Sons and Owden, was thanked for his practical sympathy and assistance, and for the free grant of the ground on which the building was erected.[45]

Reading rooms were a product of the 1880s and 1890s and most towns in Ulster had one.[46] Mechanics' Institutes, Working Men's Institutes and Temperance Institutes promoted the use of leisure time for self-improvement among the working classes. One of the aims of the Lisburn Temperance Union which was formed in 1887, with JN Richardson of Lissue as the first Chairman, was the provision of a centre with reading and recreation rooms, to counteract the attraction and evil influence of the public house. When the Temperance Institute opened in Railway Street in 1890, it contained a reading room and library. In August of that year, Mrs JD Barbour presented the library with eighty-three books and later Mrs Richardson of Killowen presented fourteen volumes of bound magazines. [47]

In both locations, at Tullynacross and Lisburn, although very different in terms of scale, we find representatives of the Richardson and Barbour families, local mill owners and landlords, committed to improving the social conditions of their workforce and very generous in providing financial support to create the facilities. It is hard to judge the success of the Tullynacross reading room after its formation, but from the minute books that survive from the 1930s and 1940s we learn that the reading material was limited to the *Belfast Telegraph* and the *Lisburn Herald* and the main emphasis was on recreation and games.[48] The members played darts, dominoes, snooker, draughts and cards, and demonstrated a proficiency at billiards. In 1932 they won the Petticrew Cup for billiards and were second in the Lisburn and District League, with J Lewis recording the highest break in the league. Their competitors included Hilden, Lisburn News-room, Temperance Institute, Dunmurry Parochial Hall, Catch-my-pal, and the British Legion at Lisburn and Dunmurry.

The 1930s were times of depression and during this period the unemployed were excused their dues, and social evenings were organised to help them and the younger members. Although the rooms were a male preserve, a Ladies' Committee helped their men folk by organising cake fairs to raise funds. The rooms were opened on Christmas Day and Boxing Day, which is a measure of the importance of the rooms as a venue for social intercourse. Concerts and socials were held and a most unhealthy sounding function, called a Smoker, was a popular form of entertainment. The building, which has long since been demolished, was a corrugated iron structure

We retrace our steps back towards the village until we arrive again at Lambeg Bridge, where we take a right turn, just past the former entrance to Coca-Cola, where the lock keeper's house originally stood.

COCA-COLA

A few words on Coca-Cola are in order. The Lambeg Bleaching site was purchased by Coca-Cola Bottlers (Ulster) Ltd in 1964 and, after extensive renovation work, The Rt Honourable Captain Terence O'Neill, Prime Minister of Northern Ireland, officially opened a new bottling plant on 22 April 1968. The plant, which had a production capacity of 50 million bottles of Coca-Cola, was managed as a family business by Terence Robinson, the son of the founder. The franchise for the production of Coca-Cola in the greater Belfast area had been awarded back in 1939 to Tom Robinson, whose business operated as the 'Ulster Iced Drinks Company', from tiny premises in Rumford Street, off the Shankill Road, Belfast. Few people in Belfast would have been familiar with this American drink, created in 1886 in Atlanta Georgia, when Dr John Stith Pemberton created a special syrup, which when mixed with carbonated water produced a distinctive drink. The drink was named Coca-Cola after two of its main ingredients, an extract of the cola leaf and the kola nut, and from the outset the trademark name 'Coca-Cola' was written in flowing Spencerian script. The recipe for the syrup is kept in an Atlanta bank vault,

The Coca-Cola Girl.
© *The Coca-Cola Company*

Buildings along the canal, 2007.

103

and only a few individuals know the formula.[58] The Lambeg plant expanded over the years and was subject to changes in ownership; it was taken over by the Dublin-based Fitzwilton group and later by the Athens-based Leventis Corporation. In 2005 Coca-Cola announced expansion plans and a move to a new site at Knockmore, Lisburn. At Lambeg some of the refurbished old brick buildings bordering the tow-path were still in use, a legacy from the former Lambeg Bleaching, Dyeing & Finishing Co. What does the future hold for this site, which is an important gateway to the Lagan Valley Regional Park?

We are going to walk along the tow-path or 'along the line' as it was called but, unfortunately, we can't offer you a rest, or a seat, before we head for Ballyskeagh. There used to be a seat here opposite the entrance to the Bleach Green where the locals often sat and played draughts, a pastime which they took very seriously, or just sat and watched the world pass by at a much slower pace than today.[59] Villagers, young and old, would meet at the bridges, and the road over the Wolfenden's Bridge was a recognised pitch for playing marbles. There was little to disturb a game of 'marlies', except perhaps, a passing horse and cart, or occasionally the Barbour's Rolls-Royce.[60]

CHAPTER 6
The Canal Walk

We commence our walk along the tow-path, following the stonewall, which is the former boundary wall of the premises of the Lambeg Bleaching, Dyeing and Finishing Co Ltd. In the photograph below, the company van is visible on the right, above the wall, as it passes the gable end of the lock-keeper's house. The gatehouse is seen in the centre, with (possibly) the gateman posing for the photographer. The upper gates of the lock are visible in the foreground, with a lighter-man on the walk board and a tow-rope laid out over the gate and along the tow-path.

Lambeg Bleaching, Dyeing and Finishing Co.
PRONI D/1770/5/3/B

Masonry arches on the side of the canal indicate the position of the two water intakes for the works. The lock keeper's house, designed by Thomas Omer, was similar to the lock-house at Drumbridge. This lock was operated over the years by John Kain (or Kane) and Billy Livingston. In 1885, William Menow was reported as being too frail and unfit for his duties here, having completed thirty years as the lock keeper.[1] The lock numbering commenced from Belfast and Lambeg was Lock 9 of the twenty-seven locks over the length of the canal.

An aerial photograph (next page) gives the layout of the Lambeg Bleaching,

Grassing linen, Nevin's Row
in the background.
PRONI D/1770/5/3/C

To our right, the wall or boundary fence follows the line of the tow-path at the start of our walk, but soon a four-bar iron fence replaces them, and we can see a full flowing drain and the green pastures of the local farms. Look carefully to the right and you will notice the grass bank that forms the earth wall to the spring fed dam that was formerly the property of the Lambeg Bleaching and Dyeing Co. Beyond this bank, the Scots pines, which make the dam look so attractive, act solely as sighting lines for you because this beautiful spot cannot be viewed from the path. Generations of Lambeg youths had no such viewing restrictions and the dam, called the Gravel Hole, was a popular place for swimming on a hot day. Look carefully and you will see the stone channel and the timber boards for the sluice on the overflow from the dam (see right). When the Bleach Green was operating, these fields to our right would have been white, covered with linen laid out on the grass. The photograph above, shows the quiet industry of laying down the sheets of linen transported there by horse and cart. The Belfast hills form the backdrop to the picture and Nevin's Row and the lock house at Ballyskeagh can be glimpsed through the trees on the right.

Our path follows the River Lagan at this point, which is one of the sections where the river and canal combine, but very soon we will follow the canal bank in a straight line when the river turns north towards Chrome Hill. We call on the Bard of Lambeg, James McKowen for a rendering of a few verses of his song about his native Lagan, which he published under the name of Kitty Connor.

The sluice.

Laying down the linen at
Lambeg Green
PRONI D/1770/5/2A

The barge *Portadown*
EHS ECA

Song – **Along The Lagan Water**

To R J, Limerick

The Shannon do you boast?
Of Barrow are you braggin'?
Then fill, and drink a toast –
Here's to my native Lagan,
Where hum the whirling wheels,
Where merry beetles clatter,
All dancing jigs and reels
Along the Lagan water.

Upon its banks, a boy,
I often dreamed and doted;
Or simply wondered why
The water lilies floated,
Or angled pike and trout,
Or tracked the cunning otter,
And found 'his lodgings' out
Along the Lagan water;
Nor heeded whirling wheels,
Nor merry beetles' clatter,
All dancing jigs and reels
Along the Lagan water.

Kitty Connor

Along this stretch of water you may be lucky and see the bright flash of a kingfisher, or the sleek otter's shadow at dusk, but you will have firm confirmation that the trout and pike are here if you see any of the patient fishermen along the bank dance a jig or a reel!

We intend to journey along the canal only as far as Ballyskeagh, which is less than a mile away, but on that short trip we can reflect back to earlier times when the canal was operational and the lighters glided back and forth from Belfast and Lough Neagh. The tow-path is punctuated here, and throughout its length, with archaeological remains, milestones from the past, which stand silently on the banks of history, refusing to fade and decay. In your imagination you can see the lighter tied up, the lighterman and the hauler taking a break and the horse grazing the canal bank. Water transport was effective: a single horse could pull a fully laden barge, weighing up to eighty-five tons. The average speed of a lighter on the canal was two miles per hour and, allowing for delays at the locks, the journey from Lisburn to Belfast took about twelve hours.

A barge, or lighter, had a crew of at least two people, one to steer the barge and the other, known as the hauler, to lead the horse. Tommy Hunter, who lived at Station Road, Lambeg, was a hauler who had a stable for his horse at the back of his house. The hauler's lot was a hard station, tramping out the miles in all weathers, all year round, with the horse for company. The horse walked along the path, pulling the barge with a long tow-rope. The path was called the towing-path, or tow-path, a term used today for any path running along the side of a river.

There are a variety of structures along the tow-path, varying from a mundane, unfinished, reinforced concrete shell known as the White Wall, or Gilmore's Folly, to the grandeur of the Ballyskeagh High Bridge. Philip Dixon Hardy (1793–1875), in his *Twenty-one views in Belfast and its neighbourhood* calls it the 'Forth Bridge' by which he meant the 'Fourth' bridge.[10] The first bridge was at Newforge, the second at Shaw's Bridge and the third at Drumbeg, making this one the fourth. Fred Hamond has stated, "historically it is of interest on account of its mid-eighteenth-century construction date … architecturally, it is arguably the most impressive canal bridge, in terms of scale and proportion, to survive in the Province. Finally, it makes a very significant impact on the landscape hereabouts." [11]

The bridge carries the road from Lambeg to Drumbeg on an S-bend over a deep cut for the canal just above the eighth lock. The canal and tow-path are spanned by arches, one broad and one narrow, built in reddish, sandstone rubble with cut stone voussoirs. Wear marks from the barge tow-ropes are visible on the central pier, which also carries a benchmark. It is said that the last person to be hanged for sheep stealing was executed at Ballyskeagh Bridge. It was a public execution and those who attended were asked if they had any messages for their friends in Hell, as the condemned man could pass them on when he arrived there.

To the side of the bridge a flight of thirty-seven steps leads to the lock

Above: Gilmore's Folly.

Below: Derelict lock house, Ballyskeagh.

EHS

Ballyskeagh steps.

The 'Forth Bridge', Ballyskeagh, from *Twenty-one views in Belfast and its neighbourhood*, 1837.

Reproduced with the permission of the Linen Hall Library

Ballyskeagh High Bridge, 2007.

keeper's house, which was built by Thomas Omer, the canal engineer, between 1759 and 1763. The attractive two-storey stone building, in Omer's individual style, is similar to the lock keeper's house at Drum Bridge. The house, which was restored by Hearth in 1992–93, is described in the Archaeological Survey of County Down as "square in plan and of two floors, built of … rubble with wrought dressings; the roof is slated … at the centre of each elevation is a recess, with semicircular arched head with key-block, rising from the platband; on the N, the recess contains a door with block architrave and square head formed of stepped and projecting voussoirs, the keystone rising to the level of the platband which is continuous across the recess; the recesses on the other elevations contain windows." [12]

The house originally afforded good views in each direction, which allowed the lock keeper enough time to attend to his lock when barges came into view. A report of 1884 suggested that this was a job for the younger man, when William Ward at Ballyskeagh changed places with his son Arthur, who operated the Mossvale lock, the

Lock house, Ballyskeagh, 2007

reason given was "the heavier duties and long climb up to the lock-house at Ballyskeagh were becoming too much for an old man." [13] The duties of the lock keepers were laid down in the Lagan Navigation Company regulations, which stated that they were responsible for watching over the banks, towing paths, locks, weirs, overflows, waste sluices, bridges and quays, and keeping in repair the banks and roads under their charge.[14] Rules governing the operation and maintenance of the locks included the lock keeper sounding his horn when a loaded lighter entered his lock, and in periods of dry weather keeping his lock gate properly secured with moss to prevent the waste of water.[15] The lock-house was bought in 1955 by a retired lock keeper, William McCue and following his death it lay empty, was vandalised, and sat as a burnt-out shell for about fifteen years.[16] Following its restoration, Hearth was presented in 1998 with an Award of Merit from the Historic Buildings Council for Northern Ireland.[17]

Returning to the tow-path, we pass under the High Bridge and notice the steelwork of the footbridge constructed in 1995 by

Lock No 8, 1925.

McLaughlin & Harvey Ltd. A few more metres brings us to the site of the former No 8 lock, now badly overgrown and dilapidated, in contrast to the 1925 photograph (above) of this lock which shows the quiet industry of a lighter discharging coal in a lay-by on a bleak December day. The lay-by served Lambeg Mills and a road led directly to the boiler house. Another photograph of No 8 lock (right), taken from the High Bridge, shows the fields where the Seymour Hill housing estate was built, with the backdrop of the Belfast hills in the distance.

Lock No 8 viewed from the High Bridge.

ILC & LM

We promised a short trip along the canal and we have now reached the point where you can turn back. Have we held your interest? If so, you may wish to join us as we leave the tow-path and return by a different route, peeling back some more layers of history on our way. Have a seat on the timber benches as you make up your mind.

If you have decided to retrace your steps along the tow-path and return to Lambeg, that is the indispensable quality of this place and this tow-path, a toing and froing,

The walled garden at Seymour Hill, 1934. Mr Moncrief, Head Gardener is on the left with Mr Duff, a gardener.

Private collection

were the last two directors of J & W Charley & Co. Colonel WRH Charley, the only son of Colonel Harold Charley, chose to pursue an army career and the company merged with Barbour's Linen Thread.

Colonel WRH Charley writing in the *Lisburn Historical Society Journal* provides some interesting information on Seymour Hill, which he describes as a large square house with four floors and continues:

Colonel WRH Charley, OBE, JP, DL.

Private Collection

> … the basement below ground level had extensive kitchens, scullery, larder, pantries, dairy rooms, wine cellars and a large servants' hall. On the ground floor the entrance hall had suits of armour standing in front of painted mural walls and there was a grandfather clock with the name William Charley in place of the numerals. To the left of the front door was the dining room, which contained the large family portraits. Behind the dining room was the cloakroom, gun room and butler's pantry. To the right was the drawing room and behind it, a comfortable morning room and library. On the first floor were the main bedrooms, dressing rooms and bathroom. The bedrooms contained four poster beds and double doors from the rooms to the landing which cut out most of the noise from the landing passages. On the top floor were the day and night nurseries for the younger members of the family and also the staff sleeping quarters. Water was pumped up to the house from a well in the centre of a large paddock in front of the house. The intermittent chuff chuff of the automatic ram could often be heard. There was a large wheel at the back door, which had to be turned from time to time to pump

water up to the roof tank. There was stabling for twelve horses in the yard. In a small field behind the house in the 1930s there lived a pony called Ginger. Ginger, clad in soft shoes, used to draw the grass cutting mower across the extensive lawns and tennis courts. He also used to pull a smart pony trap. In the summer, tennis parties were held on the four grass courts and the one hard court. [25]

We left you standing at the Green Bridge and you may well ask – what can we see today? From your present position, the answer is nothing! You may, however, wish to take a diversion at this point and follow the path to the right, which will lead you in the general direction of the house, but I would suggest that you approach Seymour Hill House from the Belfast-Lisburn road via Yew Tree Walk, or the entrance to Derriaghy Glen, which is a pleasant walk.

The Housing Trust converted Seymour Hill House into six flats, but in 1986 the house was vandalised and so badly damaged by fire that it was at risk of demolition.[26] Ownership of the listed building was transferred to Belfast Improved Houses and it was successfully restored. Colonel WRH Charley, OBE, JP, DL, reopened the house on 12 October 1990.[27] Behind the house, the former upper and lower yards were converted and adapted to mews flats, and the old walled garden was renovated and now functions as the Seymour Hill Horticultural Unit, which you should visit.[28]

DERRIAGHY RIVER

The Derriaghy River flows under the Belfast-Lisburn road and enters an attractive secluded glen with paths and bridges suitable for walking. WRH Charley describes the glen of former days: "within the grounds of Seymour Hill was a lake and a waterfall leading into a fish pond. The Derriaghy River flowed into the lake and was then divided into two mill races to work the factory water wheels. The top stream was known locally as 'Little Harry', because baby Harold Charley's pram once ran away down the drive and ended up upside-down in the river. He was none the worse for the experience. The main Derriaghy River continued down through the glen until it reached the River Lagan, a short distance away near Mossvale. The glen had well maintained paths winding through luxuriant trees, creepers and bamboo jungle areas. In the glen there was a bridge, held up by chains from the first cable layer ship to cross the Atlantic Ocean. There was also a shell grotto in the glen and for, the sporting members of the family, plenty of fishing for trout and shots to be taken at woodcock, pigeons and rabbit." [29] The glen is in public ownership and should be maintained.

OAK TREE WALK

Leaving these memories of the Seymour Hill of former days we now turn left and follow the stoned path, which is part of Oak Tree Walk, towards River Road. You will soon notice a galvanised steel seat in the shape of an oak leaf, which

The Derriaghy River.

The former suspension
bridge across the River
Lagan at River Road.

EHS

this youthful dynamic:

> A slight man with a youthful appearance, he was often mistaken for a minor when on these visits with Plunkett or Anderson. If anyone uttered a co-operative heresy, he would draw himself up, issue a lecture and identify himself as a director of the 'modest and not unsuccessful' Barbour empire at Lisburn, which led him to be known colloquially as: 'the wee man from up there'. Under his guidance the activities of the IAWS prospered, making full use of the latest technology, which included the installation of an intercom system between the offices and the warehouses at Thomas Street, Dublin, and the purchase of a motorcar early in 1912. Barbour was particularly concerned to develop the grocery trade believing that he could gain higher added value by marketing quality processed food through the co-op grocery movement at home and abroad. He believed strongly that Irish fresh food was the best in the world and needed to realise its full potential on the markets of industrial Europe. The quest for quality was on in earnest.[17]

During the Great War he financed the expense of an additional IAOS organiser to promote the cultivation of more land and during the 1916 Easter Rising he established a £3000 credit facility for the IAWS with the Ulster Bank in Belfast.[18] The main Dublin banks were closed, which caused the crisis, and the British army had occupied the IAWS headquarters in Thomas Street, which were sealed off for a week. Another generous gift to the society was a donation of £5,500 to build a new warehouse and frontage at their Thomas Street premises.[19] It was a condition of the gift that the building was dedicated to the work of the co-operative movement pioneers, Sir Horace Plunkett, Robert A Anderson and Father Tom Finlay SJ.[20] The 1918 frontage remains in place.

Harold Barbour resigned from the chairmanship of the IAWS in 1922, following the partition of Ireland, but continued to support the co-operative movement. He was elected President of the newly formed Ulster Agricultural Organisation Society in 1923 and worked tirelessly for the agricultural community and the public of Northern Ireland. He served in the Senate, which was the upper house of the Northern Ireland Parliament.[21] The duties that he undertook included Northern Ireland representative on the United Kingdom Wheat Commission, Chairman of the Joint Milk Council, Chairman of the Butter and Cream Marketing Board, Chairman of the Trustees of the Hillsborough Agricultural Research Institute, Chairman of the Council of the Young Farmers' Clubs, Chairman of the Northern Ireland Rural Development Council, Chairman of the School Committee of the Greenmount Agricultural College, member of the Pigs Marketing Board and the Co Antrim Committee of Agriculture and several of the Ministry of Agriculture's Advisory Committees.[22] He undertook all these offices on condition that he would receive no fees or salary for his services and he would not accept reimbursement of his travelling expenses.[23] It

Sir Horace Curzon Plunkett
(1854–1932).

Plunkett Foundation

is appropriate that his gravestone in Lambeg is inscribed, "He was the friend of the farmer".

"A man he was to all the country dear"

Horace Plunkett, Harold Barbour's friend, was appointed Vice-President of the Department of Agricultural and Technical Instruction, which was set up under an Act of 1899 that introduced the technical education system to Ireland. TP Gill was Secretary to the Department, which was advised by a Board of Technical Instruction that included Frank Barbour in its membership. Frank Barbour embraced this new concept and it was he who first suggested that Lisburn should have a technical school.[24] In February 1901 he wrote from the Ulster Club, Belfast, on the subject to TP Gill.[25]

Dear Mr Gill,

On my return from the meeting of the Technical Board last Wednesday I wrote to the Chairman of Lisburn Urban Council suggesting that they should take some steps to avail themselves of the provisions of the Act for Technical Education and he has asked me to attend their next council meeting and point out what advantages they can derive so I would feel much obliged if you can give me information as to what the other towns of the same population as Lisburn are doing and what are the leading features of Technical Education specially interesting to such towns. Lisburn is essentially a manufacturing town, there are four large flax spinning mills, several small weaving factories, hemstitching works etc. I believe myself that cooking class and home industries, sewing and such domestic education would be very valuable in the houses of the work people for the women, and instruction in building, mechanics, spinning, weaving and commercial book keeping, drawing etc., for the young men. If you would arrange to send down one of your organizers to explain the work that should be undertaken a good meeting could be arrange (sic) to hear him.

Yours sincerely
Frank Barbour

Lisburn Urban District Council lacked the motivation to introduce technical education and twelve years were to elapse, from Frank Barbour's original suggestion, before a school was opened in Castle House, Castle Street, which was the former residence of Sir Richard Wallace. John Milne Barbour formally opened the Municipal Technical Institute on 7 November 1914. Harold Barbour gave distinguished service on the Lisburn and Belfast Educational Committee and a plaque in Lisburn Institute commemorates his term as Chairman of the Technical Committee and refers to him as one "who was a good friend to the pupils and teachers of this school from 1914 to 1938, *A man he was to all the Country dear.*" The Barbour family members were generous in their continued support for the school and provided money to purchase textile machinery, and Mrs Harold Barbour financed the equipment for new classrooms and a laboratory.[26]

Harold Barbour married his American cousin, Anna Edwards Barbour, daughter of Robert Barbour of Paterson, New Jersey, and lived at Strathearne, a large and substantial house on the Belfast road between Finaghy and Dunmurry, which later became part of Princess Gardens School and is now part of Hunterhouse College. Harold Barbour enjoyed his work and the strength and support of his wife. In a last letter to his children he wrote, "I cannot wish you a happier life than mine has been." [27] He died at Zurich, Switzerland, on Christmas Eve 1938 and his ashes were later interred in the family vault at Lambeg. His wife, Anna, died two years later at Windy Brow, the new family home at Belsize Road, Lisburn. His eldest son, John Doherty Barbour, inherited Conway. An appreciation of his life and work published in the *Belfast News Letter*, had this to say of his character, "… a man who could be trusted, someone to whom injustice was intolerable, whose sense of fair play was inspiring and, above all, a man whose object in life was to leave his country a better place than he found it." [28]

Sir Horace Plunkett, in a letter to Mrs Barbour, expressed the personal and national debt due to them:

> There are very few people to whom I am so deeply indebted for the kindness which most appeals to me. Unlike Harold, I was an idle man with an ideal! The generosity with which you both helped me to work it out – not only the cash but the time and effort you lavished in the movement we built up – has won my lasting gratitude. I wish I could get my countrymen to realise what you have done for them …[29]

SIR JOHN MILNE BARBOUR

The Right Hon Sir John Milne Barbour, DL, MP (1868–1951), second son of John Doherty Barbour, is the Barbour family name most associated in the public mind with Hilden Mill and Conway. Educated at Harrow, Brasenose College, Oxford, and in Darmstadt, Germany, he entered the family business in 1888 and spent the next sixty-three years expanding and consolidating the firm, succeeding his father as Chairman and Managing Director of The Linen Thread Co Ltd and William Barbour & Sons, Ltd.[30] He played an important role in the development of the manufacture of netting for the American west coast salmon fishing industry and made frequent sales visits to Vancouver, British Columbia.

Rt Hon Sir John Milne Barbour, DL, MP (1868–1951), by Cowan Dobson.

ILC & LM

He realised the importance of training and the need for investment in education, to ensure that the skills needed by Lisburn's textile industries were available locally. The support given to Cecil Webb, the first Principal of Lisburn Technical School, was not simply a material one, as McReynolds points out: "Milne Barbour actually appears

OH! HERE'S
BARBOUR'S NETS
THERE'S NO ESCAPE

"Great Barbour's I'm off."
"Yes, hurry it's the Red
Hand net."

ILC & LM

to have had a considerable input into the curriculum for textile training. An example of this is the latter's suggestion that the course should include a wide variety of processes, such as preparing and spinning flax, bleaching and dyeing, plain and damask weaving, and marketing the products. He also suggested training in subsidiary skilled trades, such as mechanical and electrical engineering and millwrighting".[31] He was also supportive of those willing to learn, and his apprentices were released at four o'clock on days when they had evening classes to attend.[32] This demonstrated progressive thinking for the 1920s.

Sir Milne Barbour was a public figure of immense standing in the local area, as well as in the wider business community, and he gave a lifetime commitment to politics and the government of Northern Ireland. As an Ulster Unionist member he represented Antrim in the Northern Ireland Parliament from the General Election of 1921, and South Antrim from the 1929 election, until his death in October 1951. He was Parliamentary and Financial Secretary to the Ministry of Finance from June 1921 until April 1937; Minister of Commerce from April 1925 until January 1941 and Minister of Finance from January 1941 until May 1943. He was appointed a Privy Councillor for Northern Ireland in 1925. During his tenure in office as a Government Minister and a member of the Cabinet he did not accept a salary for his work.

The Rt Hon Sir James Craig, Bart, DL, the first Prime Minister of Northern Ireland, had great respect for the ability and endeavour which Milne Barbour brought to his post. This is clear from a private letter, triggered by Russell Scott's report on the Northern Ireland Civil Service, written by Craig in 1926 while staying at the Midland Adelphi Hotel, Liverpool, on the eve of his departure to Canada. Craig points out that any proposed changes will not diminish Barbour's position:

> *I wish to assure you that in such an event your status and position as a Cabinet Minister will not be in any way lowered, lessened or impaired; as Financial Secretary to The Ministry of Finance you would continue in control and answer questions as at present. Please do not let whatever change may be found necessary interfere with the splendid work you are doing for Ulster; we still have much to set right before we can say our duty is done and in what lies ahead I could not face with the same confidence without your valuable assistance. This is merely a line to let you know how indispensable you are.*[33]

Milne Barbour became Minister of Finance in 1941, but he had already declined the post in 1937 when Craig, by then Viscount Craigavon, offered him the position following the death of the previous Minister, HM Pollock. Barbour felt that he could not devote the time, which he knew the position demanded, and never a man for half-measures he declined the office, although Craigavon's letter offering the position had stated, "your qualifications are unquestionable and you possess the complete confidence of the whole community." [34]

An examination of other public posts held by Sir Milne Barbour provides a measure of his commitment to the wider community. He was High Sheriff of Co Antrim in 1905 and of Co Down in 1907.[35] He was a President of the Belfast Chamber of Commerce, of the Royal Victoria Hospital, and of the Royal Ulster Agricultural Society; and also a member of Belfast Harbour Commissioners and the Senate of Queen's University. In contrast, Lady Spender, the wife of Wilfred Spender, who was Secretary to the Cabinet, provides us with this odd description of Milne Barbour: "a curious man who looks like a stage Mephistopheles but is given to preaching in dissenting chapels".[36]

On 1 June 1889, Milne Barbour married his American cousin, Eliza Barbour, eldest daughter of Robert Barbour of Paterson, New Jersey, USA, who died in 1910. They had three daughters and one son, John Doherty Barbour (1906–1937). There was a landing strip at Conway, sited on the Charley land across River Road, which was used by the youthful John D Barbour, who was a keen flyer, but he was tragically killed in a plane crash at Johnstone, Renfrewshire, Scotland in July 1937, aged 31 years. In 1939, as a memorial to this young man, his aunt, Anna E Barbour, presented the Barbour Memorial Playing Fields, Lisburn, for the use of the public with the express intention that people of all ages would derive maximum benefit and enjoyment from her gift. Plaques on the memorial entrance pillars record this tribute to John Doherty Barbour: "He loved chivalry truth and honour freedom and courtesy", and this dedication, "These playing fields are affectionately dedicated in the hope that those who use them may cultivate such qualities so that the benefit of his example may not fade from amongst us."

An aerial photograph of Conway (next page) shows the rural setting of the house where Sir Milne Barbour lived for almost fifty years. He died on 3 October 1951 and is buried in Lambeg churchyard. During his memorial service in St Anne's Cathedral, Belfast, it was said of him that as "a captain of industry, he had combined outstanding

Letter from Viscount Craigavon to Milne Barbour, 19 April 1937.

Private collection

If you venture up the lane you will find only the ivy covered, decayed ruins of stone houses, the abandoned homes of forgotten generations who have faded into antiquity like their predecessors who once occupied the circular fort that was sited in this area. The fort is now destroyed and from where we stand at the roadside it is not immediately apparent that the fort commanded a strong position above the Lagan with dramatic views down the river valley. The view is shared by the neighbouring Woodland House.

CAHOONS

You will recall that earlier on our tour we recounted memories of harness racing on the Co Down side of the Lagan. Well, we are now facing the site of the original pony-trotting course, Cahoon's course. This was the first track in Lambeg and it was also used at one time for greyhound racing. It was owned by Robert Cahoon and located on land behind the former Sportsman's Inn, which he also owned. In the entrance to the pub was a painted sign announcing "The Home of the Champion Stallions King Hammer and Colonel Hammer". The Cahoon stable of horses was trained and raced in the 1920s by Dick Smith, who lived in nearby Carman's Row.[57] In harness racing circles of that day, Dick Smith was the top driver and Lambeg was the centre of horse trotting.

Jim McFarland at Robert Cahoon's, Lambeg.

Ulster Star

Church of Saint Colman, Queensway, Lambeg.

ST COLMAN'S

The Sportsman's Inn has recently been remodelled as Robbie Cahoons and the adjoining land is now church property. St Colman's Roman Catholic Church was built in 1957 and suffered an arson attack during the recent troubles. The present church, which was designed by Belfast architects Kennedy, Fitzgerald & Associates, was built in 1991. The layout of the church interior forms an effective theatre in the round, where the whole space is the worship space. Neill Shawcross, the Lancashire-born painter, who has lived and worked in Ireland since 1968, designed the stained

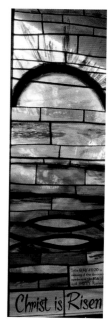

Stained glass windows at the Church of Saint Colman, Queensway, Lambeg.

glass windows, which were made in the Hilden studios of CWS Design. The altar, Presidential chair, lectern, baptismal font and the Stations of the Cross were executed to designs by Ray Carroll.[58] St Colman's school opened on the same site in 1968 and the first pupil to be entered on the general register was a James Patrick McDowell.

DERRYVOLGIE COURTHOUSE

To the left of the entrance to St Colman's, was the site of the old Derryvolgie manor courthouse, built in 1837, probably at the expense of the Marquis of Hertford. The Seneschal, Mr William Gregg, agent for the Hertford estate, held a manor court here on every third Monday, when all actions for the recovery of debts under twenty pounds British were heard and determined.[59] There were on average twenty summonses issued for each court sitting. The grand jury for the manor of Derryvolgie held a manor Court Leet in the courthouse twice a year, convened by the Seneschal's summons, when they presented sums for the repair of by-roads, pipes, fences, removal of nuisances and various other purposes within the manor.[60] The jury was composed of tenants of the manor, who taxed themselves for the sums needed to meet the purposes approved by the courts. The courthouse was maintained as a residence up until its demolition in May 2006 to make way for further housing development. At a period it served as a school, a home for two families and a single dwelling. The last occupant was Mrs Phyllis Hewitt, who lived there for almost fifty years.

Derryvolgie Courthouse.

LAMBEG MARSHALSEA

From courts, we move to prisons and offenders. A *Belfast News Letter* reward notice, from 1757, provides a detailed description of a former resident of the Lambeg Marshalsea, William Boultan, who almost killed a woman in making his escape.

> On the second instant, William Boultan, prisoner in Lambegg Marshalsea, made his escape out of said prison: He is about 5 feet 7 inches and a half high; went off in a white strait coat, an old fustian coat on the top of it, a double–breasted strip'd drugget waistcoat, a brown wig, shammy breeches, almost new, ridge and fur stockings, swarthy complection, out–mouth'd, and ill teeth. Now I promise a reward of two guineas to any person or persons who shall take and lodge him in any of his Majesty's jails in the Kingdom of Ireland, so that I may get notice thereof.
>
> Lambegg, March 3, 1757.[61]

Newspaper advertisements, which offered a reward for information leading to the apprehension of offenders, were common in the eighteenth century. The following example refers to trespass and malicious damage at Lambeg House:

> Whereas some evil minded covetous and malicious person or persons have of late trespassed on the farm and lands joined to Lambeg House, by breaking the fences, driving on cattle, stealing young trees, flowers, and flowering shrubs, and otherwise abusing the premises; and to complete their unprovoked villany, on the night between the 17th and 18th instant, broke several of the windows of the said house in a shocking manner.
>
> Now this public notice is given, that if any person is found trespassing on said concerns for the future, that they will be prosecuted with the utmost severity; and if any will discover and prosecute to conviction the above thefts, a reward of two guineas, and for the breaking of windows, the sum of ten guineas shall be paid by
>
> Wm: Nevill
>
> Lisburn, 18th February 1767.[62]

... and this one to desertion from the army by a Lambeg man:

> Deserted from Major Balaguier, recruiting for Col. Pole's Regiment, Andrew Allen of the town and parish of Lambeg in the County of Antrim, 5ft 8in, fair hair, slender made, a shoemaker by trade, and commonly called the Young Sovereign. Whoever secures the above Deserter and lodges him in any of his Majesty's goals, and gives notice to Major John Balaguier at Belfast or Lisburn, shall receive 20*s*., over and above the 20*s*. allowed by Act of Parliament for apprehending Deserters; but if after this notice he delivers himself up to me, he shall receive his pardon

HARMONY HILL PRESBYTERIAN CHURCH

William Moore was a tall and distinguished looking man, who was a well-known local character. A Presbyterian, he walked every Sunday to First Lisburn Presbyterian Church in Market Street, where he was an Elder. Harmony Hill Presbyterian Church, which we passed at the bottom of the hill, was opened in 1965 to cater for the local Presbyterian congregation. Designed by Munce & Kennedy, and built at a cost of £35,820, the building has been described as a tent, and uses basic, simple materials for its construction – painted brick walls, pine boarded ceiling and a concrete floor. The screen behind the pulpit is constructed in concrete and finished with a bronze polish. The church bell in the tower is from a different era and has a history; it came from Clogher Presbyterian Church in Co Mayo, bears the date 1874 and carries the crown, a harp and the shamrock. The Mayo church was demolished in 1931 and the congregation no longer exists.[13]

William Moore on his 'seat'.

Gallery window detail, Christ Church, Derriaghy.

INGRAM

Many fine houses surrounded Lambeg and the cottages on Harmony Hill were between two of these houses. Above the row of five, white-washed cottages was the entrance to Ingram, a house that had been rebuilt in 1828 by the Reverend John Corken (c1798–1834).[14] The new house was a commodious, five-bay square building, two storeys high and slated, with an oblong wing attached to the east side.[15] Trees sheltered the house and yards and the area in front of the house was neatly laid out with shrubberies and gravel walks. Iron railings bordered the gravelled entrance drive. In 1819 the Rev John Corken married Maria Cupples (1797–1881), daughter of the Rev Snowden Cupples, Rector of Lisburn Cathedral.[16] They had three sons and three daughters. Maria Corken survived her husband by forty-seven years and in 1872 she dedicated the Gallery window in Christ Church, Derriaghy, to his memory and that of her three sons, who are all buried in the churchyard. A daughter, Elizabeth Anne (1833–1923), married Matthew Johnson-Smyth, a solicitor. When Maria Corken died in 1881, she was again living at Ingram, which was to become a Johnson-Smyth property.[17]

Maria Corken (1797–1881), daughter of the Rev Snowden Cupples, Rector of Lisburn Cathedral.

THE JOHNSON-SMYTH FAMILY

Ingram, which was set in a demesne of thirty-four acres, was the home of Jonathan Richardson (1804–1894) and Margaret Airth (1807–1889) who lived there for almost twenty years.[18] When the Richardsons moved to Lambeg House about 1847, Ingram was occupied by the Corken and Johnson-Smyth families. The Johnson-Smyth family had a long association with Lisburn and the wider area.[19] Their original surname was Johnson, to which the additional Smyth surname was added after the death in 1788 of Edward Smyth, brother-in-law of the Reverend Thomas Johnson. Rev Thomas Johnson, who was Curate of Lisburn, Master of the Latin school in Lisburn and Vicar of Magheragall 1742–1757, married Mary, sister of Edward Smyth, who, by his will dated February 1787, bequeathed property and money to three of his Johnson nephews with the request that they take the additional surname Smyth. It would appear that two brothers complied with the request, Roger Johnson-Smyth and Lt Col Matthew Johnson-Smyth, but the Reverend Phillip Johnson, Curate of Lisburn and Vicar of Derriaghy 1772–1833, retained the surname Johnson.

We will concentrate our attention on Roger Johnson-Smyth (1744–1816) and his family, for it was his descendants who came to live at Ingram. Roger appears to have lived in Halifax, Nova Scotia, for a period and his wife Lydia was described in a 1795 death notice as "a native of North America, and came lately to reside in this kingdom". They are buried in Lisburn Cathedral graveyard. Their eldest son Thomas Johnson-Smyth JP, DL (c1785–1860), who was Deputy Lieutenant for County Down, married Charlotte Bruce of Kilroot, Co Antrim, by whom he had four sons and two daughters. His eldest son Roger, who lived in Castle Street, was elected MP in the 1852 election when the independent electors of Lisburn nominated him in opposition to Lord Hertford's candidate. Up until that time, Lord Hertford had nominated the candidates and this was the first attempt by the Lisburn electors to secure the independence of the borough when Roger Johnson-Smyth (1815–1853) stood against John Inglis, the Lord Advocate of Scotland. Roger Johnson-Smyth's political career was brief; he never married and died suddenly in August 1853, in his fortieth year.[20] His father, Thomas Johnson-Smyth, had previously suffered a tragic loss when another son, Lieutenant Thomas Johnson-Smyth, RN, of her Majesty's frigate *Juno,* lost his life when aged 29 years, in a heroic attempt to save the lives of a boat's crew upset in the surf, off the coast of California in May 1846.[21] He is commemorated on a memorial in Lisburn Cathedral. Another son of Thomas Johnson-Smyth was the Reverend Edward Johnson-Smyth MA, Vicar of Glenavy 1852–1885. A fourth son, Matthew (1818–1865), was a solicitor. In 1854 he married Elizabeth Anne Corken (1833–1923), referred to above, youngest daughter of the Reverend John Corken, Vicar of Aghalee, and had two sons and a daughter, Thomas Roger, Matthew Bruce and Maria Frances McNaughton, known as Minnie.

MAJOR THOMAS ROGER JOHNSON-SMYTH

Major Thomas Roger Johnson-Smyth (1857–1900) was born in June 1857 and educated at Rossall School, Lancashire. He played rugby for Lisburn in the early days when rugby was introduced to the town as a sport. On entering the army, he was based in Dublin and joined Landsdowne rugby club where he soon attracted attention for his style of play. He was described as "one of the finest exponents of the old Irish forcing game", at that time a distinctive feature of international matches, which led to his selection in representative games and an Ireland cap in 1882 in a home international against England at Lansdowne Road.[22] This was a game that aroused some controversy, although it was the best result yet against England. Ireland had lost the five previous internationals between the two countries and on this occasion it was a draw, two tries each, but that was not how some critics saw it. This was long before we had action replay and a fourth official. You saw it once and this was how the journalist Jacques McCarthy reported the result.[23]

> Without any possibility of contradiction, Ireland won by a goal and a try to two tries, but the official result was a draw. This was the famous Pike cum Nugent match, Pike the player winning it, while Nugent the umpire lost it. McLean kicked a goal for Ireland off a try by Taylor, but Dr Nugent decided that it was no goal. Stokes scored for Ireland immediately after the kick-off, but Walkington missed the kick, then Hunt got in for England, Rowley missing. WN Bolton (an Irishman by the way) then scored for England and finally M Johnson got a try which was virtually scored by Taylor. Off this McLean kicked the goal referred to and which was disallowed by Nugent amidst universal dismay.[24]

Major Johnson-Smyth joined the 106th Foot, from the Antrim Milita in 1878. He served with the Soudan Frontier Field Force, 1885–86, and was present in the engagement at Giniss, receiving the medal and Khedive's Star. In 1899 he embarked for South Africa with his battalion and served with the Natal Field Force. He was mentioned in despatches. Major Johnson-Smyth was killed in action during the Boer War, while leading his men of the 68th Regiment, 1st Battalion, Durham Light Infantry at the action of Vaalkrans on the Upper Tugela River, on the 5 February 1900. The remains of the British soldiers who fell at Vaalkrans have been re-interred in the Garden of Remembrance sited on the southeast slope of the hill. Major Johnson-Smyth, whose grave was located near the Tegula, has also been re-buried there. The obelisk erected to the memory of the 1st Durham Light Infantry lists the names of twenty-one fallen and a marble cross has been erected to the memory of Major Johnson-Smyth. He is also commemorated on a tablet in the nave of Lisburn Cathedral, erected by his widow, and a memorial window in Christ Church, Lisburn. At the request of the *Lisburn Standard*, Samuel Kennedy

Memorial window, Christ Church, Lisburn.

The Richardson's Bessbrook mills and factories worked in conjunction with the Glenmore Bleach works and the Richardson, Sons, & Owden, Ltd, warehouse in Belfast. John Grubb Richardson married secondly Jane Marion Wakefield of Moyallon, Co Down, in 1853, and settled at Brookhill, outside Lisburn; later the family removed to Moyallon House, the home of his wife's family.[6] They had one son and seven daughters.

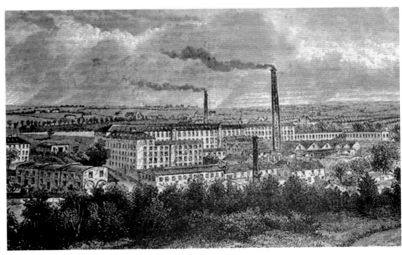

Bessbrook Mill.

John Grubb Richardson was a man of principle, a philanthropist and, in political terms, liberal in outlook. He withdrew from the Inman shipping line, which he had helped found, when it provided supply vessels for the Crimean War[7]; he approved the scheme for Unsectarian National Education[8]; supported the Irish Land Acts[9] and at all times cared for the welfare of the people of Bessbrook. In 1882, John Grubb Richardson declined a Baronetcy offered by the Prime Minister, WE Gladstone and extracts from the correspondence relating to the offer give an insight into his character.

Downing Street
April 21, 1882.

Dear Sir,

I have received the permission of Her Majesty to offer you a Baronetcy. It gives me much pleasure to propose to you an honour which I trust will not be disagreeable to you; and your acceptance of which will I am confident gratify all those who have had an opportunity of appreciating your personal position and your public services.

I remain, Dear Sir,

Faithfully yours,

WE Gladstone[10]

The Woodhouse,
Bessbrook, 4 th Mo. 24,
1882.

Dear Mr Gladstone,

I have duly received your kind letter offering me by permission of our beloved Queen the title and position of a Baronet for which I feel grateful as if I could accept the offer. You are aware that I belong to the Society of Friends, some of whose members in early days resigned their titles for conscience's sake. I cannot say I feel as strongly as they did in this matter, but I feel as if the acceptance of your offer on the grounds of having tried to do a little for the benefit of my fellow men would detract from the satisfaction I have found in so doing . . .

Believe me to be
Yours faithfully
John G Richardson.[11]

The letter declining the offer continued, with JG Richardson urging Gladstone to adopt some plan for the furtherance of the Temperance cause.[12] It was his firm belief that much of the country's misery was due to the misuse of alcohol and religious animosity and, if these could be stamped out, another cause for disturbance, political agitation, by men who made politics a means of personal gain, could be eliminated.[13] Jane Marion Richardson in *Six Generations of Friends in Ireland* states, "Caring as he did for the welfare of his fellows belonging to every class and creed, the extremes of party feeling were particularly distasteful to him. To heal the wounds of Ireland and repair her waste places was his dearest wish."[14] We must leave John Grubb Richardson with his wish unfulfilled.

JAMES NICHOLSON RICHARDSON

John G Richardson's young son from his first marriage was called James Nicholson Richardson (1846–1921) and in later life he fondly reflected on his time at Lisnagarvey House, as he recalled: "Aunt Malcolmson, it seems to me in looking back, must have had a special gift for bringing up young people. She was the only person in authority over me whom I never remember to have disobeyed, and who never, so far as I recollect, directly ordered me to do, or not to do anything."[15] James spent a lot of time in his father's company, riding out with him almost daily and enjoying a degree of freedom. He leaves us this descriptive picture of himself riding in this area: "Mounted on an ugly but most docile pony, 'Clove', followed by a dog, 'Rollo', and sometimes with a fond cockatoo on my shoulder, I was allowed, within certain limits, to ride about at will." [16] James N Richardson had a distinguished career, representing Armagh as a Liberal MP in 1880 and succeeding his father as Chairman of the company, a position he retained until his death in 1921.

Sarah Malcolmson died in 1864 and her youngest sister, Anna R Pim (1827–1906), widow of Joshua Pim of The Glen, Whiteabbey, continued to maintain open house at Lisnagarvey for any Richardson family members in need of help or support. She merited an inclusion in *The Quakri at Lurgan*, with these lines, published in 1877 by James N Richardson, that young boy who, twenty-eight years previously, first came to stay at Lisnagarvey House.

> There stept a stately matron forth
>
> As e'er bore Quakri name.
>
> Yea, had good Anna Pimlia lived
>
> In Rome's most goodliest days,
>
> Both great and poor had called her 'friend,'
>
> The bards had sung her praise.[17]

Anna R Pim (1827–1906).

Anna Pim lived at Lisnagarvey House until her death in 1906, when her children, brother and sister, Goff and Laura Pim, occupied the house. James N Richardson had this to say about his cousin Laura Pim: "Laura is a wonderful woman, so quiet and yet so capable … She runs that large place inside and outside and carries on a great variety of good works – Friends' work and other – with apparent ease. No wonder I wrote about her long ago in *The Three Auburn Queens*." [18] Lisnagarvey House was the setting for an annual garden fête, one of the major social occasions attended by all the families in the area. A marquee was set up in the grounds and fancy goods and cakes were sold from the stalls. Tea and refreshments were served in the glasshouse while the local Lisburn band provided musical entertainment on the lawn. The gardens of Lisnagarvey House provided a local source for vegetables, apples, tomatoes and cooking apples, which were purchased from the gardener.

Lisnagarvey House offered their stables as a store for Friends' School equipment and property in 1940 when the Ministry of Public Security requisitioned the school as a temporary military hospital. Laura Pim declined to make the house available for senior girl boarders, who were eventually accommodated in Ardfallen, Fort Hill, when Winifred Graham was persuaded to leave her home and move to Finaghy.[19] The house was later converted to a residential home and then in 1968 the property was sold for a housing development.

BELSIZE

Just off the Belsize Road, above Lisnagarvey House, stood the 'Rookery', the name for several two-storey tenement type buildings located down a separate access lane, at the back of Belsize farm. The basic standards and life style that prevailed here were in sharp contrast to life in the big house. The Rookery was eventually destroyed in a fire. Where did the name Belsize come from? Based on information provided by

Lisburn and established a successful drapery business in Bow Street. William and Ester Chittick had often admired Elmwood while out walking and one day they called to enquire if the owners would consider selling. The Paynes accepted an offer of £3,000. Originally from an agricultural background, WJ Chittick maintained his connection with the land by running a farm enterprise from Elmwood, with poultry and a herd of beef cattle, taking additional land from neighbouring estates as required. Chittick's family business traded as ladies and gents outfitters in Bow Street for seventy-five years and closed in 2006.[54]

PARKLANDS

We have arrived at the bottom of the Belsize Road and, just before we reach Parkmount, we notice the house on the right called Parklands.

DR J G JOHNSTON

Dr JG Johnston moved to this house in 1949. Born at Mahee Island, Co Down, in 1884, Joseph Greenfield Johnston was educated at the Royal Belfast Academical Institution. He graduated MB, BCh in 1908, proceeding MD in 1913,

Parklands, 2007.

and entered general practice in Lisburn in 1910. He operated from his home at 46 Castle Street,[55] which he called Clovelly House after the North Devon village, on account of the 155 steps from the basement to the top floor, a name he transferred to Belsize Road. A single storey wing to the house acted as a dispensary, where he made up his own cough mixtures, medicines and tinctures.

During World War I, Dr Johnston served with distinction with the 36th Ulster Division, 108th Field Ambulance, Royal Army Medical Corps. He had been a medical officer in the UVF and joined up on the formation of the Ulster Division; serving at the Somme, Cambrai and St Quentin.[56] He attained the rank of Lieutenant Colonel and was awarded the Military Cross in the 1918 Birthday Honours List, having been previously mentioned in despatches.[57] He married Norah Mary Wilkins at a registry office in London, in 1916, while on leave on a ten-day pass. A present to the couple from the Field Ambulance unit of six silver spoons, inscribed St Omer, Armentières, Albert, Amiens, Ypres and Hazebrouck, was a poignant reminder of his war service. Dr Johnston was President of the Lisburn branch of the British Legion, but he seldom spoke of his war experiences and never discussed them with his family. He proudly

Dr JG Johnston.

King George VI is accompanied by Lieutenant Colonel Dr JG Johnston MC, the President of the Lisburn British Legion, during an inspection of members of the British Legion in Market Square in July 1937, the coronation year. Queen Elizabeth is escorted by JD Barbour, the Chairman of Lisburn Urban District Council.

ILC & LM

escorted the Prince of Wales (later Edward VIII) at a review of ex-servicemen in 1932 and King George VI and Queen Elizabeth at an inspection of local members of the British Legion in Market Square in July 1937, the year of their coronation.

On demobilization, Dr Johnston was appointed surgeon to the County Antrim Infirmary and later also surgeon to the Lisburn and Hillsborough District Hospital (now the Lagan Valley Hospital). These appointments he held until the introduction of the National Health Service in 1948. He retired from general practice in 1969. He was President of the Northern Ireland Branch of the British Medical Association in 1948 and, in 1951-52, President of the Ulster Medical Society as well as finding time to serve for periods on many other committees.[58] In his address to the BMA he outlined the history of county infirmaries and drew on his predecessor's "interesting if lurid account" of the infirmary in Seymour Street. That account we find even more interesting, when viewed with the benefit of our experience of present day standards of medical care and equipment.

The staff consisted of a Matron who was not a trained nurse, two nurses, neither of whom could either read or write and who had received no training whatsoever, and a porter. There was no night nursing at all. One of the nurses occupied a bed in the female ward and the porter slept in one of the male wards. The Dispensary was the abode of very large black and grey slugs and cockroaches and the yard was infested with rats. There was one bathroom with the bath sunk in the stone-flagged floor and seldom if ever used. Behind the hospital were the pig-styes from which a stream of sewerage found its way down the yard, and flies were plentiful.

The Operating Room had a wooden table and a wooden press holding instruments, and at each end a human skeleton. In the wards there was no ventilation, except when the windows were open, which was seldom. The beds were iron and the mattresses, straw stuffed into ticks. The plates were wooden, and knives and forks were not provided. There were no wash-basins and taps, vermin were plentiful, especially bugs. In this year he records that there were forty operations performed, with four deaths, perhaps not too bad a result under the conditions prevailing.

In 1885, the first attempts at modernisation were made viz., the building of extensive bathrooms and lavatory accommodation. In 1887, a trained nurse was appointed as Matron and nurses were instituted in place of the attendants on the sick as previously. Also, in the same year, the change of the mattresses from straw to wire-woven was a great advantage, rendering the wards cleaner and the air purer, as the debris of the straw when the beds were made floated about in the air. He advocated, however that thin hair mattresses over the wire ones would be of service as the wire was rather cold to lie on in the winter. In 1893, we have reported: – the amount of stimulants used during the year was four-and-a-half gallons of whiskey, thirty-nine dozen of stout and a gallon of gin. No wonder the man and the place were popular! In 1896, a horse ambulance was provided by public subscription in the town for the removal of sick people and accident cases to the hospital.

In 1904, electric light was provided by means of a petrol driven engine and dynamo, and the first X-ray plant was presented to the hospital by the Barbour family.[59] This was a small machine that made a terrific noise: there was a visible spark of some 6-12 inches, and although I was present at its use on several occasions, I must confess its workings were a complete mystery to me, and I was terrorised by this exhibition of intern thunder and lightening. In 1912, a new operating theatre and sterilising room were built, and an electric lift installed, and so, gradually, we see a comparatively modern hospital with most of the amenities for up-to-date treatment evolved from this primitive house of discomforts, insects and dirt, within the lifetime of one individual.[60]

Dr Johnston was a strong and athletic young man with an interest in rugby football, but a promising future in the sport was disrupted with the outbreak of war. He played for Lisburn FC and was selected to represent the Provincial Towns Clubs in

1913, and in January 1914 he was in the Ulster junior inter-provincial panel against Leinster.[61] Outside medicine, Dr Johnston was involved in another theatre with the Lisburn Choral and Orchestral Society. He had a detailed knowledge and love of the Gilbert and Sullivan operas and his fine baritone voice allowed him to take part in performances playing lead roles; Wilfred Shadbolt in *Yeomen of the Guard,* Don Alhambra in *The Gondoliers* and The Lord Chancellor in *Iolanthe.*[62] Gilbert and Sullivan was the subject of his Presidential address to the Ulster Medical Society in 1951.[63] Dr Johnston moved to Forthill in his final years and died on 5 January 1971, aged eighty-six years. He was buried in Lambeg churchyard. His presidential address to the BMA concluded with a poem, which he gave as the epitaph of the country surgeon. Two verses serve the same purpose for Dr JG Johnston, MC, MD, JP

> The Doctor sleeps. His fighting days are done,
> But hundreds live because of bouts he won,
> And, generations hence, those who draw breath
> Who would not Be had he not vanquished Death.
>
> The Doctor sleeps. Might we his deeds recall
> His name would blaze in Fame's enmarbled Hall,
> But serving modestly through life, it now seems best
> To merely write, "His work survives", and let him rest.[64]

Derek G Johnston, the eldest son of Dr JG Johnston, moved into the family home on Belsize Road. Derek, the well-known BBC motoring correspondent, was the winner of the 1952 Circuit of Ireland Trial, in an MG TD.[65] In 1956 he was a member of the winning team in the Monte Carlo Rally; in those days a test of endurance run over narrow twisting roads and contested largely by amateur drivers.[66] The car, a Jaguar Mark VII, was supplied by the factory, but there was no back-up or support from the company, and the team were very much on their own.[67] Ronnie Adams of Lisburn and Frank Bigger from Dublin were the other members of the team, which won the premier award, the Prince Rainier Cup, and a prize of £1,200.

The house was sold later to the Abbeyfield Lisburn Society. It is currently named Parklands and functions as a sheltered housing scheme. We have reached the bottom of the Belsize Road passing Parkmount on the right, and just opposite, also with a view over Wallace Park, we have the terraces of Park Parade.

Derryvolgie

DERRYVOLGIE

Moving along, we approach Hilden bend and a mature belt of trees to our left heralds the entrance to Derryvolgie, currently in use as offices of the Department of the Environment, Water Service, but in a neglected state pending the privatisation of the service. Derryvolgie House was the seat of William Gregg, one of Lord Hertford's agents, who built Derryvolgie about 1835.[22] The house was a neat square two-storey building with a slated roof, well-enclosed yard and good offices at the rear.[23] Set in twelve acres, the demesne

was laid out in well-enclosed fields and was improved by creating plantations of various kinds of forest trees.[24] The plantings reflected Mr Gregg's good taste and in the *Ordnance Survey Memoirs* Thomas Fagan commented that the place was almost new, but went on to forecast that in a few years it would be one of the healthiest and handsomest seats along the Lagan.[25] Originally the elevated site commanded "a most delightful prospect of the handsome and well improved valleys, extensive bleach greens and numerous gentlemen's seats in its neighbourhood, also of Lisburn, Hillsboro' and a wide extent of the counties of Antrim and Down." [26]

WILLIAM GREGG

William Gregg, JP (1797–1870) was the son of Dominick Gregg (c1764–1826), a Quaker, and one of the old linen merchants of Lisburn who, together with John Hancock and others, was instrumental in starting a movement for the repeal of the law which made bleach green robbery a capital offence. William Gregg played an important role in the life of the district. He was agent for Lord Hertford's estate and as Seneschal of the manors of Killultagh and Derryvolgie he presided at a manor court held each month in the court house, Lisburn, and another at Derryvolgie court house.[27] He was in the Commission of the Peace for upwards of thirty years and he was never known to overstretch his magisterial power on the Bench or elsewhere.[28] He was responsible for summoning the grand juries for the manor of Killultagh and the manor of Derryvolgie to hold a court leet twice a year.[29] Gregg served on the committee appointed in 1833 to superintend the building and management of the new fever hospital. He was an honorary member of the Killultagh Hunting Club, which met monthly in the Hertford Arms Hotel to make arrangements for the hunts and transact items of general business.[30] The hounds were hunted twice a week on Wednesday and Saturday.[31] William Gregg married Anne Fulton Caldbeck in Lisburn Cathedral in April 1831, but she died three years later, aged 24 years.[32] William died in February 1870, aged 73, and is buried with his wife in the Cathedral graveyard. William Gregg left the Quakers, but five of his unmarried sisters were life-long members and are buried in the Friends' Burying Ground in Railway Street. Derryvolgie was left to his unmarried sisters and following the death of Miss Anna B Gregg, the last survivor of the family, the house was sold in 1898.[33]

THE EWART FAMILY

It is the Ewart name that is commonly associated with Derryvolgie House, but the business empire created by this great linen family was based in Belfast, although its origins can be traced to Carnreagh, near Hillsborough, where Thomas Ewart had a lease of a twenty-acre farm in 1716.[34] The Ewarts distributed locally spun yarn to neighbouring cottage weavers and sold the finished cloth to the bleachers.[35] Thomas Ewart's grandson, William, born 1759, had greater ambitions and about 1790 he moved to the village of Ballymacarrett outside Belfast, where female labour was plentiful.[36] He taught the people there to weave on looms, which he had installed, and purchasing yarn in the local yarn markets he began to finish and sell his own cloth.[37] By 1814 William Ewart (1) (1759–1851) had taken his eldest son, also called William (2) (1789–1873), into partnership and the firm of William Ewart & Son was established with an office and warehouse in Rosemary Street, Belfast.[38] The firm continued to expand, buying and building spinning mills, weaving factories and warehouses to meet the worldwide demand for its products. In the 1840s the firm acquired ground, with water rights, on the Crumlin Road, Belfast, where they built their first spinning mill, adding a power-loom weaving factory in 1850 and building a new modern mill nearby in 1868. The next generation had entered the business and with William Ewart (3) (1817–1889) having joined the partnership in 1843, for a period the partners were father, son and grandson. William Ewart (3) was one of the outstanding figures in the life of Belfast. He was Mayor in 1859 and 1860 and represented the city at Westminster from 1878 to 1889.[39] He was one of the deputies from Belfast for the arrangement of a treaty of commerce with France in 1864 and was created a baronet in 1887. In 1883 William Ewart converted the firm to a Limited Liability Company, with capital of £500,000.[40] He and his sons were the first directors.

Derryvolgie House became Ewart property when Frederick William Ewart (1858–1934), the sixth surviving son of Sir William Ewart, bought the house in 1898.[41] He made many additions and improvements.[42] FW Ewart DL, MA was educated at Wadham College, Oxford and was called to the Bar, King's Inn, Dublin, in 1888.[43] He was for many years a District Inspector in the Royal Irish Constabulary but eventually he became Managing Director and later Chairman of William Ewart & Son, Ltd.[44] The Ewart family had, over a number of years, taken an interest in the well being of the Church of Ireland and FW Ewart was no exception. A diocesan report refers to him as one "whose devotion to the interest of the church was fervent and whose wise advice was always looked for and relied on. His balanced judgement and courteous helpfulness have been of inestimable service, and won not only the esteem but the veneration of all. He represented a family that has from one generation to another enjoyed to a unique extent the gratitude of Belfast church people." [45]

Following the death of FW Ewart in 1934, Derryvolgie passed to his eldest son, Major Gerald Valentine Ewart RASC (1884–1936), a Director of the firm.[46] FW Ewart had two other sons who were also members of the firm and served in the Great War. Captain Cecil Frederick Kelso Ewart (1888–1916) was educated at Winchester. He was a company commander with the 1st Lisburn Battalion, Ulster Volunteer Force, supplying his men with rifles and ammunition and allowed them to conduct target practice on his own private shooting range.[47] In February 1915 he was commissioned in the Royal Irish Rifles and in October he embarked for France from Bordon Camp with A Company, 11 Royal Irish Rifles (South Antrim Volunteers). He was promoted to Captain early in 1916. He was second-in-command of C Company and took over the command when Captain Samuels was wounded on 1 July 1916. Captain Ewart was killed in action that same day near Thiepval Wood on the Somme, aged twenty-eight years.[48] His death is commemorated on the Thiepval Memorial, France, and in Christ Church, Lisburn.[49] The Thiepval Memorial also commemorates the death of Rifleman James Andrews from Hillhall Road, Lisburn, a member of the UVF, who acted as orderly for Captain Ewart and was killed in the same action.[50] Major William Basil Ewart (1890–1920), who died

Captain Cecil FK Ewart (1888–1916).

ILC & LM

197

Grand Street Mill, Paterson, New Jersey.

ILC & LM / Zirkus

and Slater Street, they proceeded thereon to erect the finest specimen of mill architecture in New Jersey, if not in America. In the Spruce and Grand Street mills nearly 1500 hands are employed, who produce over 200,000 dollars' worth of finished goods every month. They import the flax just as it comes into the market from the farmers in the north of Ireland, and in the Paterson Mills they spin it into all kinds of linen thread, shoe thread, sewing thread for tailor's uses, fine twine, etc. They also dye and bleach it on their own premises. They spin thousands of miles of thread every day. If every man, woman, and child in America used a spool of Barbour's sewing thread in the course of a year, the Paterson Mills alone could supply them. They do produce far more than that quantity. But the shoe thread is the greatest demand, being used in preference to any other, all over the country. They have their principal store and office in New York City.[18]

In Lisburn, Grand Street and Spruce Street were named after the mills and streets in Paterson, New Jersey. The Barbour's characteristic insistence on quality and durability in the standard of architecture of

Spruce Street Mill, Paterson, New Jersey.

ILC & LM / Zirkus

their mill buildings at Hilden was transferred across the Atlantic to the building operations there. The new Grand Street Mill, erected in 1877, had a frontage of 50 feet and a depth of 250 feet and stood four-storeys high.[19] The light coloured brick courses at intervals made it ornamental as well as useful. The mill was fitted with a sprinkler installation supplied from a pond on Garnet Mountain. The mill had scarcely been brought into production, using machinery shipped over from Ireland, when it was decided to increase the floor space and it was then extended by 50 feet. Ten years later the building was again extended in length, to 500 feet. The old mill in Spruce Street was rebuilt following a fire in February 1879 and followed the design of the Grand Street Mill. In 1881 they built another mill called the Granite Mill, after the material used in its construction.[20]

Thomas Barbour was a giant of a man, not only in the physical sense but also in the business community. He was the first President of the Paterson Board of Trade, a Director of the Guardian Fire Insurance Co of New York, a Director of the Hanover National Bank and a Director of the Paterson and Ramapo Railroad Company.[21] In addition to his home in Paterson, he had a summer residence at Brookside Farm and a country seat outside the city at Warrenpoint in Bergen County.[22] A newspaper report said of him: "He was a man genial in manner and the very embodiment of hospitality and influence; when any question arose demanding unusual energy, he was never found unequal to the emergency of the case." He entertained lavishly at Warrenpoint and President Ulysses S Grant was one of a number of prominent people who were invited there as his guests.[23] Thomas Barbour had a fondness for whisky and by the 1880s, probably because of this, he was to some degree estranged from his wife. His overseas trips became more frequent and, as we already know, it was on one of these trips that he died at The Fort. William James Barbour, born 1828, the third son of William Barbour, was a doctor by profession and practiced in the County Antrim Infirmary, Lisburn before he went to America and settled in Quincy, Illinois.[24] There is a suggestion that William James was the black sheep of the family and received a remittance from them to stay out of Ireland.

LISBURN ELECTION 1863

You will remember meeting with John Doherty Barbour, the eldest son of William Barbour, on our walk past Conway, which he bought in 1892; but prior to that time he had lived at Hilden House and The Fort. John Doherty Barbour was highly regarded as a successful businessman, but his venture into the political arena remains a blemish on his character and Hilden House became the stage for the most absurd farce. It took place in 1863 when Barbour stood in a parliamentary by-election for Lisburn, caused by the resignation of Jonathan Richardson, who had represented the Borough from 1857. Barbour stood as a Radical and the man selected by the Lisburn Tories to stand against him was Edward Wingfield Verner, the son of an

John Doherty Barbour (1824–1901), eldest son of William Barbour.

ILC & LM

estate owner from Co Armagh. Verner was proposed by Jonathan Richardson of Glenmore and seconded by Redmond Jefferson of Bow Street. Barbour was proposed by Hugh McCall, pawnbroker, and seconded by James Mussen, Cross Row, a calico seller. The franchise was restricted to those occupiers of property with a valuation of £8 or more and there were 313 electors on the list for that year. Before the 1872 Ballot Act the element of secrecy had not been introduced for the ballot box and each voter publicly declared for a candidate and everyone knew how he had voted. Booths were erected in Market Square for the voting procedure.

Bribery and corruption was commonplace and candidates would attempt to 'buy' votes with cash payments or promises of gain. It was against this background that John Doherty Barbour set out to win the 1863 election, but the tactics he employed plumbed new depths even for that period. Prior to the election John Doherty and his brother, Robert, took over Hilden House and converted it into a holding centre where twenty voters were detained to ensure that they honoured their commitment to vote for Barbour. The *Belfast News Letter* of the day gives us an account of the amusements provided for the detainees during their incarceration.

> A portion of the premises of Messrs. Barbour was prepared as a sort of a garrison to which voters were carried off by fair means or foul and where, for nine days, they were kept in a state of jovial incarceration eating, drinking, fiddling, dancing and card playing. The windows were nailed down lest any man should escape. A guard of nine men armed with muskets gently coerced the imprisoned electors. The garrison was supplied with food brought on the carts of Messrs. Barbour and if the voters had only got beds in which to sleep off the effects of drink of the weariness of jigging to the perpetual fiddles they would have nothing to complain of.[25]
>
> … so the fiddling and card playing and dancing were on and the sentinels held stern guard at the gates and save for an occasional alarm that 'the enemy was coming to rescue them', the garrison had a splendid time of it. The voters were marched to the polls two by two, a doubtful man always linked with one who was all right and who threatened to 'knock his eye out' if he did not vote for Hilden where he had been so hospitably entertained.[26]

Two of those held at Hilden, John Brady and Thomas Corry, were expected to impersonate their dead fathers, whose names were still on the list of electors. The Barbour faction dragged the sons up to the poll, but the Verner supporters were aware of the intended deception and when the impersonators were put on oath they withdrew in shame. John Rea, a Belfast solicitor, published a caustic account of the actions of some of those 'persuaded' to vote for John Doherty Barbour and gave details of the graft and corruption and sums of money expended by Barbour to procure votes.[27]

over time everything in this photograph has been obliterated in the name of progress!

We cannot stand in the way of progress, but we can influence future development plans and their impact on the urban landscape and the environment. During the tour we have learned something of the history of the district and made the acquaintance of the people who once lived here

Empire Sunday, Lambeg Corner.
SCC

and contributed to the growth, improvement and prosperity of the area. Generally they were men and women of substance and property and, having passed on, we can see the faded imprint of their presence on the landscape and the shadow of their contribution to the built heritage. Have we, as individuals, a contribution to make? What legacy will we leave for the benefit of future generations? We can begin by conserving the link with past generations and appreciating their values and achievements. We can foster a sense of civic pride and encourage the formation of community interest groups to take action to protect our heritage and surroundings. Local history is on our doorstep. Look around and you will be amazed at the list of opportunities that present themselves.[59]

An interest in local history should encourage us to value the district in which we live and, by finding out about the past, we generate a feeling of continuity with what has gone before and the people who lived in this place over time. It can foster a sense of identity, and an understanding of that distinctiveness will strengthen and enrich the community. Each generation contributes to the history of the local area and each of us has an opportunity to add to the recorded history. Local history is about people and places and if your people came from this place in the past, then you should find it comforting to follow a path that was once familiar to your forefathers. Walk alone through the village, along the roads or the tow-path and take a moment to reflect on times past, their times, and see their lives woven into the pages of general history; recall those private memories from the past, the fragments of family history known only to you and set them down as a record, a guide for others who may be interested to pass this way, if only through the pages in a book.

Notes

Chapter I, Lambeg Village, pages 9-42

1   JAK Dean, *The Gate Lodges of Ulster – a Gazetteer*, 1994, p 15.

2   George Hill, *An Historical Account of the MacDonnells of Antrim*, 1873, appendix II, p 385.

3   'Origin and Characteristics of the People in the Counties of Down and Antrim' in the *Ulster Journal of Archaeology*, Vol 1, 1853, p 249.

4   Henry D Inglis, *A Journey Throughout Ireland during the Spring, Summer and Autumn of 1834,* London, 1836, p 355.

5   Rev John Dubourdieu, *Statistical Survey of the County of Antrim*, 1812, p 484.

6   Angelique Day & Patrick McWilliams (eds), *Ordnance Survey Memoirs of Ireland, Vol 8, Parishes of County Antrim II 1832-8*, p 134.

7   Ibid, p 141.

8   Ibid, p 134.

9   Sequoyah (c 1770–1843) also known as George Guess or Gist, was born in the Cherokee Nation in Tennessee to an English father and a Cherokee mother. A hunter, fur trader, warrior and silver smith, Sequoyah began work on a Cherokee alphabet around 1809. After considerable effort he realised the difficulties and complexities and concentrated instead on developing a syllabary, a system in which the syllables of a spoken language are represented by phonetic symbols. Sequoyah settled on a syllabary of eighty-six characters and in 1821, he demonstrated his invention before the Cherokee national council by exchanging messages with his young daughter. Within a few years most Cherokees had become literate in their own language. Sequoyah later supplemented the Syllabary with a Cherokee numerical system. Source: *The Oxford Companion to United States History*.

10 "The most visually significant trees on the site are the small grove of nine Giant Sequoias. While these are recorded as nine trees, eight of these are off-shoots from the centre parent tree created by branch 'layering' many years ago". Source: Tree Survey by Estate & Forestry Services Ltd, Oct 1990.

11 Day & McWilliams, *Ordnance Survey Memoirs*, op cit, p 138; H C Marshall, *The Parish of Lambeg*, 1933, p 114.

12 James Beck, 'The Williamsons of Lambeg' in *Flax and Linen, Rise of the Linen Merchants, Fibres & Fabrics Journal,* Dec 1942, pp 59-61, contains an account of John Williamson and the Williamson family.

13 HC Marshall, op cit, p 114; A commentary by Fred Heatley and Hugh Dixon on Lambeg House, plate xxi, in EK Proctor's, *Belfast Scenery*, 1832, (Linen Hall Library reprint), refers to John Williamson purchasing Lambeg House in 1760. The following notice from the *Belfast News Letter,* 4 March 1760, indicates that Lambeg House was to let in May 1760 and could be sub-divided: "to be let from the first of May next Lambeg House, with the office houses, &c. and any quantity of land that may be wanted, not more than thirty acres – or the front house, which is complete in itself, will be let separately, with such office houses and land as may be wanted. The garden and land may be entered upon immediately. Proposals to be received by John Hancock at Lisburn, or John Williamson at Lambeg. Dated 4 March 1760".

14 Hugh McCall, *Ireland and her Staple Manufactures*, 1870, pp 72-73.

15 Ibid.

16 Ibid, pp 74-75.

17 Ibid, p 78.

18 Ibid, p 80.

19 The *Belfast News Letter,* 30 Oct 1764, referred to in the *Ordnance Survey Memoirs,* op cit, p 142.

20 The *Belfast News Letter,* 15 July, 26 July 1765; *Freemans Journal,* 27 July 1765.

21 The *Belfast News Letter,* 25 March, 27 May, 11 Nov, 9 Dec 1766.

22 Ibid, 26-30 July 1776.

23 Ibid, 9 Oct 1767, contains John Williamson's obituary notice.

24 Day & McWilliams, *Ordnance Survey Memoirs*, op cit, p 139; HC Marshall, op cit, p 115.

25 The *Belfast News Letter,* 18-22 May 1795.

26 Ibid, 24 June 1784.

27 Neville H Newhouse, *A History of Friends' School Lisburn*, 1974, p 1; PRONI Greer family letters D1044/850, microfilm.

28 William Nevill married in June 1753, Anna Hancock, sister of John Hancock, Snr. He was one of four executors named by John Hancock, Snr, in his will. His bankruptcy was the immediate cause of a serious family and Quaker dispute, when Betty Hancock, mother of John Hancock Jnr, who

was fearful that Nevill's creditors would claim against her son's estate, corresponded with a large number of Ulster Quakers. Nevill, in a letter to Lisburn Monthly Meeting, acknowledged his past misconduct and admitted that a "too eager pursuit of worldly concern" had led him astray. Opposition to Nevill remained strong and an attempt to kidnap him in Dublin in 1777, by Quintin Dick, was bungled when he escaped after being held captive for two hours. Source: Neville H Newhouse, 'John Hancock Jnr 1762-1823' in *Journal of the Royal Society of Antiquaries of Ireland*, 101, 1971. The following advertisement by Hancock Nevill, son of William Nevill, of Lambeg is of interest. "To all such persons of both sexes (more especially the hungry and naked) that are out of employment, whose indigence arises not from a disposition to indolence, and whose inclination leads them to America. Hancock Nevill, son of William Nevill, of Lambeg, intends going to the Province of Pennsylvania early this spring with Francis Exton, merchant in Philadelphia, and taking with them a number of servants. Therefore all such, whether tradesmen or labourers, &c. from 10 to 30 years of age, who can be well recommended, have consent of their parents, and willing to indent themselves for three to seven years, according to their age, to serve in said Province, where they may expect relief from their present indigent condition, and by faithful service obtain a future happy settlement; may apply to William Nevill at Lambeg, or at Lisburn, Hillsborough, and Belfast on Market Days; or to Francis Exton, at the Cross Keys, North-Street, Belfast, who will take care of such as are agreed with to have them well provided at sea, new clothed, and disposed of to humane masters. 21 Feb.1774". Source: The *Belfast News Letter*, 4-8 March 1774. A further notice informed passengers bound for Philadelphia with Hancock Nevill to board the *Peace and Plenty*, Captain McKenzie, at Belfast on 5 May 1774. Source: The *Belfast News Letter*, 22-26 April 1774.

29 Neville H Newhouse, 'John Hancock Jnr 1762-1823', in *Journal of the Royal Society of Antiquaries of Ireland,* Vol 101, 1971, p 41; The *Belfast News Letter,* 8 Dec 1770, contains a notice referring to the property of Hancock and Nevill stolen off the bleach green at Lambeg; The *Belfast News Letter,* 9-13 Aug 1776, refers to William Nevill's interest in the one half of the bleach green and utensils of Lambeg, during the minority of J Hancock, the younger.

30 The *Belfast News Letter,* 9-13, 20-23 Sept 1774.

31 Ibid, 25-29 Aug 1775.

32 Neville H Newhouse, 'John Hancock Jnr', op cit p 43.

33 Neville H Newhouse, *A History of Friends' School Lisburn,* op cit, pp 23-24.

34 Robert Scott, *A Breath of Fresh Air The Story of Belfast Parks*, 2000, p 199.

35 Neville H Newhouse, John Hancock Jnr, op cit, p 49.

36 Ibid.

37 Ibid.

38 Ibid.

39 *Belfast Monthly Magazine*, Feb 1812, p 93. The article is signed 'K'.

40 Joseph R Fisher, *Royal Belfast Academical Institution*, 1913, p 204.

41 *Journal of the Statistical and Social Inquiry Society of Ireland*, Vol IX, 1896.

42 Thomas Hancock, *The Principles of Peace*, 1825, pp 96-97.

43 *Belfast Monthly Magazine*, Vol 1, 1809, p 138.

44 Jean Agnew & Maria Luddy (eds), *The Drennan – McTier Letters 1802-1819*, Vol 3, p 167.

45 In a letter to the Editor, signed 'K', Hancock refers to the scarcity in 1800 and 1801. "The cause of the scarcity in those years is to be traced to the deficient harvest of 1799, which owing to the lateness of the spring and the wet of the summer and harvest, failed in producing the usual supplies, so that the stocks of the small farmers were soon consumed by their own families and they were altogether dependent on the market for their provisions afterwards…" *Belfast Monthly Magazine*, Vol 2, 1809, p 14.

46 Hugh McCall, *Some Recollections of Hugh McCall, Lisburn*, 1899, Appendix.

47 Neville H Newhouse, John Hancock Jnr, op cit, p 47.

48 The *Belfast News Letter,* 30 Sept 1823 (from the *Commercial Chronicle*).

49 Ibid.

50 Neville H Newhouse, John Hancock Jnr op cit, p 52.

51 Henry Bell, *A short Visit to Ram's Island, Lough Neagh, and its vicinity in the year 1853*, 1853, p 20.

52 John Moore Johnston, *Heterogenea*, 1803, p 126; *Ordnance Survey Memoirs*, op cit, p 139.

53 Theodore C Hope, *Memoirs of the Fultons of Lisburn*, 1903, p 58; "James Fulton m, 10 November 1783, Ann Bell, the event being thus recorded in the *Belfast Mercury* or *Freeman's Chronicle* of the 11th idem: - 'Married last night, at Lambeg, Mr James Fulton to Miss Bell, daughter of Henry Bell, Esq, of Lisburn, a young lady who (exclusive of a large fortune) is possessed of every accomplishment to render the marriage state truly happy'. In the baptismal